Vishwanathan

Normalization of Japanese-Soviet Relations

Normalization of Japanese-Soviet Relations

1945-1970

Savitri Vishwanathan

THE DIPLOMATIC PRESS

TALLAHASSEE, FLORIDA

PUBLISHED BY

THE DIPLOMATIC PRESS, INC.

1102 Betton Road

Tallahassee, Florida 32303

© 1973 The Diplomatic Press, Inc.

Library of Congress Catalog Card No. 70–186317

ISBN 910512–16–7

PRINTED AND BOUND IN THE UNITED STATES

ROSE PRINTING COMPANY, INC. TALLAHASSEE

To my parents

Preface

Geographic closeness breeds special interests between nations. Hence, even before Japan opened her doors to the West, she had to reckon with the presence of Russia. After Japan ended her policy of seclusion, Russia was a factor which played an important role in her foreign policy calculations.

Japan realized very early that rivalry among the powers could be utilized to strengthen her own position. However, it was also brought home to her forcibly by Russia in 1895 that she should have an alliance with one of the big powers in order to conserve her gains in foreign policy. Economic and military might alone would not assure international acceptance of her achievements. Since learning this bitter lesson, Japan has been protecting her interests with the support of one of the big powers; she has had no qualms in changing her alliance partner, depending upon the circumstances.

Japan's strategic geographical situation vis-à-vis Russia and China by itself gave her special importance in American and British policies in the Far East, even before conflicting ideologies threw the Western Powers and Russia in opposite camps. Commodore Perry was prophetic when he anticipated the confrontation of the Saxon and Cossack on the eastern shores of Asia. The sense of competition between the United States and Russia over Japan, which was revealed at the time of opening of the country, came into the forefront again at the end of World War II. The Russians lost the race the second time.

In examining the relations between Japan and the USSR since 1945, this study emphasizes: (1) the role played by the American-Soviet conflict in conditioning Japan's Soviet policy as well as her domestic developments; (2) the attempts made by the USSR to draw Japan into her own fold; and (3) the domestic compulsions which influenced Japan's policy towards the USSR. I have tried to determine whether in the postwar era, Japan was just a pawn in the American-Soviet conflict or whether she did try to formulate a positive policy towards the USSR on her own independent judgment.

This book is an outgrowth of my doctoral dissertation, "Japan's Relations with the USSR, 1945–1963", submitted to the Jawaharlal Nehru University (School of International Studies) in 1970. The work is based to a large extent on Japanese language sources; all the translations from the Japanese are my own. Japanese names are written with the surname first, the personal name second. All newspaper references are to morning editions unless otherwise indicated.

My principal thanks go to Dr. P. A. Narasimhamurthy, my thesis supervisor and Head of the East Asia Department in the School of International Studies, Jawaharlal Nehru University, for his perceptive advice and criticism. I am grateful to Dr. A. Appadorai and Dr. M. S. Rajan, former Directors of the Indian School of International Studies as well as Dr. V. P. Dutt, former Head of the East Asia Department (now Pro-Vice Chancellor, University of Delhi) for giving me an opportunity and providing facilities to take up research in this field. I am thankful to all the staff members of the Library at Sapru House for the unselfish way in which they gave their time in assisting me to locate books and materials.

I should express my gratitude to the Japanese Ministry

of Education for granting me a scholarship from April language in Tokyo. This enabled me to undertake systematic courses in Japanese language at the Tokyo University of Foreign Studies. At the same time, the stay in 1966 to September 1968 for the study of Japanese Japan facilitated the collection of materials for my dissertation and gave me an opportunity to have discussions with scholars and acquire firsthand information about Japan. Subsequently, as a lecturer in the Department of Chinese and Japanese Studies of the Delhi University, I visited Japan for the second time from March to April 1971, at the invitation of the Government of Japan. I am also grateful to the Japanese Ministry of Foreign Affairs for supplying me with some of the photographs and maps used in this book. The Embassy of Japan in New Delhi also helped me with materials and I take this opportunity to express my thanks. I should also thank the Embassy of the USSR in Tokyo and the *Nisso Kyokai,* Tokyo, for assisting me with photographs and materials.

I am indebted to many in Japan for advice, encouragement and information. Among them, I should single out Professor Enoki Kazuo of the Toyo Bunko, who never turned down my requests for assistance. I owe a great deal to Professor Maruyama Masao (formerly of the Faculty of Law of the Tokyo University), who encouraged me to discuss with him all aspects of Japanese politics and gave me the benefit of his deep knowledge. I should also thank Professor Matsumoto Shigeharu, Chairman, Board of Directors, International House of Japan and Professor Nagai Michio (now on the Editorial Board of *Asahi Shimbun*) for the kind interest they took in me and for the useful discussions I had with them.

I take this opportunity to record my thanks to Professor Hugh Borton and Professor James William Morley of Columbia University for their valuable suggestions. I am particularly indebted to Professor George Alexander Lensen of the Florida State University for his useful suggestions as well as his continuous encouragement to publish the dissertation as a book.

I am grateful to the staff of the National Diet Library, Tokyo, especially their Newspaper Clipping Section, for their assistance. Thanks are also due to the staffs of the Library of the Faculty of Law, Tokyo University, the International House of Japan, and the Reference Library in the United States Embassy at Tokyo for their help.

Finally, I wish to thank my family, to whom this book owes much.

SAVITRI VISHWANATHAN

Delhi
January 1973

Contents

ILLUSTRATIONS
(pp. 52–59)

Map of Japan: Northern Territories 1970

Map of the Northern Islands

Map showing areas prohibited for fishing

Photographs:

Prime Minister Hatoyama Ichiro

Foreign Minister Shigemitsu Mamoru

Minister of Agriculture and Forestry Kono Ichiro

Ambassador Matsumoto Shunichi

Signing of Trade and Payments Agreement

Signing of Ninth Fisheries Agreement

Ambassador Oleg Troyanovsky at the Japan-Soviet Society

Fifteenth Convention of the Japan-Soviet Society

Signing of the Basic Agreement for the Construction of the port of Vrangel.

Vishwanathan

Normalization of
Japanese-Soviet Relations

Introduction

Japan enjoyed her dream of isolation for one hundred years from 1639. The first nudge to rouse her from this dream was given in 1739 by two Russian ships, sighted off the coast of Nagasa County in the province of Awa (Chiba Prefecture) and on the west coast of Ojika County in Mutsu Province.

Although the subsequent Russian attempts to open up Japan for commercial relations were unsuccessful, they created a breach in the seclusion policy and brought home to the Japanese their own weakness.[1] Japan started paying more attention to her coastal defence. The wave of Russian encroachment stimulated the interests of the Shogunate in its northern territories, viz. the Kuriles and Sakhalin. Sakhalin was absorbed as Japanese territory in 1805 after the findings of a commission.[2] The need for proper delineation of the frontiers with Russia was realized. The Japanese drafted a letter to the Russians stating that Etorofu and the islands to the south were under Japanese sway; Shimushiru and the islands to the north were to be Russian territory with Uruppu as a buf-

---

1. For a detailed account of Russian attempts to open up Japan, see G. A. Lensen, *The Russian Push Toward Japan* (Princeton, 1959).

2. J. W. Hall, *Tanuma Okitsugu 1719–1788; Forerunner of Modern Japan* (Cambridge, Massachusetts, 1955), pp. 101–4; James Murdoch, *A History of Japan: The Tokugawa Epoch, 1656–1828* (London, 1926) vol. 3, pp. 513–14; Yosabura Takekoshi, *The Economic Aspects of the History of the Civilisation of Japan* (London, 1930), vol. 3, pp. 181–87.

fer zone between them. However, the letter was not con-
veyed to Russia.[3]

While the major force behind the early Russian thrust
had been that of merchants, adventurers and scholars, the
czarist government's interest was aroused in Japan with
the increase in the British gunboat diplomacy in China
and the expectaton of American expansion in the Pacific.
With the competition of other European nations for the
commercial opportunities in China, Russia had already
lost her exclusive position there. While it was becoming
clear that she could not be the only power to have relations with Japan, she could at least make a better bargain
by being the first in the race. Russia might have achieved
her end if she had put up a show of military might, because the Japanese official circles were beginning to
understand from events in China that a policy of vacilla-
tion and procrastination would not keep out the foreigners
forever, but would rather bring the thunder of European
military might upon them.

There was an important group in the Japanese political
circles who felt that Japan might make concessions to
Russia in return for help against other countries.[4] This is
borne out by the promise given to Vice-Admiral Evfimii
V. Putiatin on his arrival on 21 August 1853 in Nagasaki
that Russia would be given priority in the matter of trade
agreements.[5] But the outbreak of the Crimean War slowed

3. The Governor of Matsumae had been instructed to hand over
the letter to the Russians. But Vasilii Novotskii, who cruised along
Etorofu in 1812, did not take the trouble to contact the Japanese.
(Lensen, *Russian Push Toward Japan*, pp. 260–61; Takekoshi, p.
192).

4. W. G. Beasley, *Select Documents on Japanese Foreign Policy
1853–1868* (London, 1955), p. 24.

5. The imminence of an American expedition to Japan hastened
the dispatch of Vice Admiral Putiatin in 1852. Still the Americans

Russian efforts and Commodore Matthew C. Perry succeeded in concluding the first treaty with Japan at Kanagawa on 31 March 1854. Thus began the long history of confrontation between the Saxon and the Cossack on the eastern shores of Asia, a rivalry of which Japan was quick to take advantage.

Russia's geographic propinquity gave her a special place in Japan's foreign policy deliberations. From the first, the delineation of the frontiers and the determination of the ownership of Sakhalin and the Kurile Islands were issues as important as the granting of commercial privileges. The Treaty of Shimoda, signed on 17 February 1855 with Russia, included a clause dividing the Kurile Islands between Japan and Russia. Etorofu and the islands to the south continued to remain under the jurisdiction of Japan, while Uruppu and the islands to the north became *de jure* Russian territory. Sakhalin was left unpartitioned.[6] The settlement was altered by the Treaty of St. Petersburg on 7 May 1875. The whole of Sakhalin became Russian territory; the entire Kurile Archipelago, Japanese territory.[7] However, the rich mineral resources in Sakhalin caused renewed friction in later years, as did the occupation of the strategic Kurile Islands by the Soviet Union in 1945.

---

beat the Russians in the race. Commodore Perry sailed into Edo bay in July 1853. Putiatin was promised priority of treatment verbally as well as in a note sent on 3 February 1854 before the Japanese plenipotentiaries returned to Edo for instructions from the Shogunate. (G. A. Lensen, *Russia's Japan Expedition of 1852 to 1855* [Gainesville, 1955], pp. 62–65; Takekoshi, p. 322.)

6. For the text of the Treaty of Shimoda and the explanatory articles see Lensen, *Russia's Japan Expedition,* pp. 122–25. Article II of the treaty discusses the territorial settlement.

7. For the text of treaty, see Lensen, *Russian Push Toward Japan,* pp. 501–6.

The mixture of fear and respect which Japan held for Russia in the early years of their relations turned into distrust once it became clear that Russia would always be an obstacle to her expansion in Asia. Rivalry became the key note in their relations. With the help of Germany and France, Russia blocked Japanese acquisition of the Liaotung peninsula and thus of a foothold on the continent as the result of her victory in the Sino-Japanese War. She also thwarted Japanese plans in Korea by interfering in Korean politics herself.[8]

Outmanoeuvred by Russia, Japan allied herself with Great Britain, which was equally interested in curbing Russian expansion. With the Anglo-Japanese Alliance isolating Russia from Germany and France, Japan successfully challenged her old rival in the Russo-Japanese War of 1904–1905.

By the Treaty of Portsmouth, which was negotiated through the good offices of the United States, Japan obtained Southern Sakhalin, the lease of the Liaotung Peninsula, including Port Arthur and Dalny (Dairen), and the section of the Chinese Eastern Railway south of Changchun, but Russia was not eliminated from North Manchuria.

Unable to assert her superiority in war, Russia evolved a policy of cooperation. Without actually becoming pro-Russian or repudiating the Anglo-Japanese Alliance, Japan worked in concert with Russia for a decade, the cordiality in their relations reaching its highest point in 1916 with the signature of the Secret Convention.[9] For

8. Andrew Malozemoff, *Russian Far Eastern Policy 1881–1904* (Berkeley, 1958), pp. 27–40.
9. For the text of the Convention of 1916, see Victor Yakhontoff, *Russia and the Soviet Union in the Far East* (London, 1932), p. 379.

a brief time it looked as if Russia and Japan would make the Far East their exclusive domain.

The Bolshevik Revolution once again cast Russia and Japan into opposite camps. Quick to take advantage of the chaos created by the revolution and by the absorption of the Allies in the war with Germany, Japan attempted to establish her hegemony in China and in Siberia. She was foiled in her efforts by American and British restrictions.

With the revolution a new dimension was added to Russo-Japanese relations—the threat of Communism. While the Soviet Union, in the early years, launched a policy of appeasement and cooperation towards Japan in order to safeguard the Communist revolution in Russia and to implement her policies of internal reconstruction, the Comintern stepped up its activities in Japan with a view to realizing the long-term goal of destroying Japanese imperialism.

By 1925 the USSR obtained the evacuation of Japanese troops from North Sakhalin and *de jure* recognition of the Soviet regime.[10] Although she failed in her efforts to woo Japan away from the Western Powers in order to knock a hole in the "capitalist encirclement," she succeeded in preserving peaceful relations with Japan. Japan derived many benefits from Soviet appeasement: the neutrality of the USSR during the Manchurian Incident, sale of the Chinese Eastern Railway by the USSR to Manchukuo, fisheries concessions, and oil and timber concessions in North Sakhalin.

While this façade of mutual amity was being maintained, Japan disclosed her true intentions by signing the

10. For the text of the Basic Convention, see G. A. Lensen, *Japanese Recognition of the USSR* (Tallahassee, 1970), pp. 177–95.

Anti-Comintern Pact with Germany on 25 November 1936.[11] Although the public articles of the pact called only for mutual help in curbing Communist activities, a secret protocol provided for mutual consultations in all matters relating to the Soviet Union and contained a promise not to give relief to the Soviet Union, if either country was threatened or attacked by the latter. In short, the pact was a limited alliance against the USSR.

The Soviet Union responded by stiffening her attitude in the matter of fishery concessions, but faced also with a threat from Germany, she was not completely obdurate. Every year she agreed to a one-year renewal of the concessions.

The rivalry and hostility of Japan towards the USSR abated when she realized that it was the United States which was thwarting her grand designs in the Pacific. On 13 April 1941 Japan concluded a Neutrality Pact with the USSR. As a price for the pact, she assented in principle to the liquidation of her coal and oil concessions on Sakhalin within six months.[12] Forewarned about the impending attack by Germany in June 1941, the USSR wished to keep her eastern frontiers quiet, and exhibited extreme cordiality toward Japan when the Neutrality Pact was signed. Japan did not appreciate the significance of this at the time.

Immediately after the Pearl Harbour attack the United States had asked for Soviet engagement of Japan in the

11. Text in Royal Institute of International Affairs, *Documents of International Affairs, 1936,* (London, 1937), pp. 297–99; Secret protocol in Germany, Foreign Office, *Documents on German Foreign Policy 1918–1945,* Series D. Vol. 1 (London, 1949), p. 734.

12. Nobutaka Ike, *Japan's Decision for War: Record of the 1941 Policy Conferences* (Stanford, 1967), pp. 21–22. Text of the Pact in Harriet L. Moore, *Soviet Far Eastern Policy 1931–1945* (Princeton, 1945), pp. 200–201.

north. Repeated attempts made by President Roosevelt to obtain Soviet cooperation in the Far East ended in failure. Although there were no more proposals to this effect by the President after 30 December 1942,[13] hope of eventually obtaining Soviet participation in the Pacific War persisted.[14]

During the course of the war both the Soviet Union and Japan spared no efforts to keep the eastern frontier quiet, each dreading an attack by the other.[15] But in 1943, when the tide of battle had definitely turned against Japan, Stalin, on his own initiative, promised at the Moscow Conference and again at the Teheran Conference that the USSR would enter the war against Japan within three months after the defeat of Germany.[16] When Stalin made his first commitment, the Soviet Union was bearing the major brunt of the German attack and the opening of the second front by the United States and Britain still seemed remote. Stalin may have thought that this commitment would ensure a quick opening of the Anglo-American second front or he may have felt that noninvolvement in the Pacific theatre of war might deprive him of a voice in shaping the future of the Far East. In his talks with Harry Hopkins in May 1945, Stalin disclosed that he wanted a say in what was done

13. USSR Ministry of Foreign Affairs, *Correspondence between the Chairman of the Council of Ministers of the USSR and the President of USA and the Prime Minister of Great Britain during the Great Patriotic War of 1941–1945* (hereafter *Correspondence*) (Moscow, 1957), vol. 2, pp. 47–48.

14. John R. Deane, *The Strange Alliance* (New York, 1947), p. 47.

15. Ike, pp. 58–121; Japan, Ministry of Foreign Affairs, ed. *Shusen shiroku* (Tokyo, 1952), pp. 1–21, 71–72.

16. Cordell Hull, *The Memoirs of Cordell Hull* (London, 1948), vol. 2, p. 1309; United States, Department of State, *Foreign Relations of United States: Conferences at Cairo and Tehran*, hereafter cited as *Cairo and Tehran Papers* (Washington, 1961), p. 147, p. 489.

about Japan and that he expected the Soviet forces to share in the occupation of Japan.[17]

American military plans for the Pacific operations assumed eventual Soviet participation.[18] Stalin's oral promises were translated into written agreement at the Yalta Conference in February 1945. Stalin had told Ambassador Averell Harriman on 14 December 1944 that he expected the return of the Kuriles and South Sakhalin to the Soviet Union; the leasing to the USSR of the southern part of the Liaotung Peninsula, including Dairen and Port Arthur; and joint Soviet-Chinese operation of the Chinese Eastern Railway from Dairen to Harbin, thence northwest to Manchuli and east to Vladivostok.[19] He had not asked for an American commitment at that time, but at Yalta he insisted that these political conditions were essential to make the Russian people understand the national interest involved in going to war against Japan. President Roosevelt promptly agreed to the demand for the southern half of Sakhalin and the Kuriles. While admitting the Russian claim for the use of a warm water port at the end of the South Manchurian railroad, the President stated that he would prefer Dairen being made a free port under an international commission rather than passed outright to the Soviet Union. Similarly, he wanted the Manchurian railways placed under a commission composed of one Chinese and one Russian. Roosevelt indicated that Marshal Chiang Kai-shek's ap-

17. United States, Department of State, *Foreign Relations of the United States: Conference of Berlin (Potsdam) 1945*, hereafter cited as *Potsdam Papers* (Washington, 1960), vol. 1, pp. 41–47.

18. United States, Department of State, *Foreign Relations of the United States: Conference at Malta and Yalta 1945*, hereafter cited as *Yalta Papers* (Washington, 1963), pp. 388–400.

19. *Cairo and Tehran Papers,* pp. 378–79, 369–71.

proval would have to be obtained for the concessions in Manchuria.[20]

The divisional committee of the State Department had prepared two memoranda on the territorial questions in the Far East. One, written by George Blakeslee on the Kuriles, had pointed out that Japan had a strong claim to the Southern Kuriles on the basis of nationality, self-determination, geographic propinquity, economic need and historic possession and that their transfer to the USSR would create a situation which "a future Japan would find difficult to accept as a permanent solution." But it had realized that since the possession of the Northern and Central Kuriles by the USSR would give her free passage into the Okhotsk Sea, the Soviet claim to these islands would be difficult to resist. The second memorandum, written by Hugh Borton, had warned also that while the USSR would have a strong claim to South Sakhalin, Japan might be embittered by its loss, because the products of the island would be of great importance to her peacetime economy.[21]

Unfortunately for Japan the above memoranda had somehow been deleted from the presidential briefing book. Roosevelt, therefore, regarded the concessions demanded by Stalin as reasonable; after all, they constituted little more than the restoration of Russia's pre-1905 rights in the area.[22] Roosevelt probably had no qualms in firmly committing himself to the cession of South Sakhalin, as under the Cairo Declaration it could be termed a territory which Japan had taken by violence and greed

20. *Yalta Papers*, pp. 768–70, 894–97. Text of the agreement on p. 984.

21. *Ibid.*, pp. 379–88.

22. *Ibid.*, pp. 768–71; William Leahy, *I Was There* (London, 1950), p. 373.

and "from which therefore [she] should be expelled."[23] This was not true of the Kuriles, however, nor of the Manchurian railroad, Port Arthur, or Dairen. While it is true that the latter had changed hands from Russia to Japan, they were basically Chinese domain. But perhaps the recognition of Soviet economic stakes in Manchuria, with the qualification that Chinese sovereignty would be preserved, was a better solution than "to abandon the cradle of conflict to the winds of fate."[24]

To refuse Stalin's conditions would have meant to conduct the Pacific War without Soviet assistance. The combined Chiefs of Staff had agreed that the war in Europe was not likely to end before 1 July 1945, and that even with Soviet aid the war in the Pacific might last eighteen months after the defeat of Germany.[25] Soviet aid in the Pacific seemed to promise the "hope of getting home alive and quickly" and this was "one of the political realities which shaped the Yalta Agreement."[26] Furthermore, American hesitation to accept the Soviet conditions for participation in the Pacific War might have induced the USSR to make a bargain with Japan, as Japan would have been ready to offer much to keep the USSR neutral.

Soviet participation in the Yalta and Teheran conferences had aroused Japanese fears that the USSR might promise to assist the Allies in the Pacific War. By 1944, the war had definitely turned to the disadvantage of Japan and she had to drain the Kwantung Army of its best divisions for the defence of the homeland, replacing them

23. Text of the Cairo declaration in *Cairo and Tehran Papers*, pp. 448–9.

24. William Appleman Williams, *American Russian Relations 1781–1947*, (New York, 1952), p. 277.

25. *Yalta Papers*, pp. 827–33.

26. John L. Snell, ed. *The Meaning of Yalta: Big Three Diplomacy and the New Balance of Power* (Baton Rouge, 1956), p. 202.

with ill equipped and poorly trained reserve divisions. In case of an attack, the operational plan of the Kwantung Army envisaged a retreat from Northern and Central Manchuria, with a last stand to be made in the southeast and along the Korean border.[27] Japan was anxious, therefore, to receive assurances from the Soviet Union of her continued goodwill.

On 5 September 1944 War Minister Sugiyama Gen supported Foreign Minister Shigemitsu Mamoru's proposal at a meeting of the Supreme Council for the Direction of the War to send an envoy to the USSR to promote goodwill between the two nations. Shigemitsu anticipated that Japan would have to make the following concessions to the Soviet Union in order to bring her into the war on their side, or if this were not possible, to restrain her from participating in the Pacific War: (1) Unrestricted navigation through the Tsugaru Straits; (2) abolition of the Japanese-Soviet Basic Convention of 1925; (3) abandonment of the fishery concessions; (4) transfer of the North Manchurian (Chinese Eastern) Railway; (5) tolerance of Soviet activities in China, Manchuria and other Japanese areas; (6) recognition of Inner Mongolia and Manchuria as within the Soviet sphere of influence; (7) abolition of Japan's defence alliances; (8) abrogation of the Tripartite Alliance and the Anti-Comintern Pact; (9) transfer of South Sakhalin; and (10) transfer of the Northern Kuriles.[28]

The Army Chiefs were willing to go along with these concessions, but as the USSR turned down the Japanese suggestion of sending a special envoy, on the grounds

27. Royal Institute of International Affairs, *Survey of International Affairs: Far East 1942–1946,* hereafter cited as *Survey,* (London, 1955), pp. 134–35, footnotes 1 and 2.
28. *Shusen shiroku,* pp. 156–64.

that there were no outstanding problems and that such a mission would give rise to unnecessary doubts at home and abroad,[29] Japan could not convey to the USSR what concessions she was prepared to make. It should be noted, however, that the above concessions included only the Northern Kuriles, not the Southern Kuriles.

After the Yalta Conference, Japan once again tried to receive assurances from the USSR that the Neutrality Pact would not be abrogated. The Soviet Union avoided giving a clear answer. On 5 April 1945, she denounced the Neutrality Pact, promising, however, that the two countries would enjoy neutral relations till the expiration of the pact in April 1946.[30]

The denunciation of the pact made Soviet entry into the Pacific War imminent. The Japanese Army believed that the Soviets would strike when the Americans invaded Japan proper.[31] Once again the Army induced the Foreign Ministry to use diplomacy to keep the Soviet Union out of the Pacific War; it also felt that Soviet good offices should be sought to end the war on terms favourable to Japan. In return, they were prepared to agree to the restoration of the general situation that had existed prior to the Russo-Japanese War of 1904–1905, provided autonomy for Korea would not be included. War Minister Anami Korechika was confident that the USSR would not wish Japan to be weakened too much in view of the possible confrontation with the United States in the postwar world.[32]

29. *Ibid.*, pp. 164–66.
30. *Ibid.*, pp. 264–66.
31. *Ibid.*, pp. 237, 266–67, 320, 558, Annex, pp. 2–4.
32. *Ibid.*, pp. 328–40, 406. A consensus was reached after discussions between the Big Six (the Premier, the War and Navy Ministers, the Army and Navy Chiefs of Staff, and the Foreign Minister) in meetings held between 11–14 May 1945 and 18 June 1945. A

In the talks initiated with the Soviet Ambassador Jacob Malik to convey the proposals of the Japanese Government, Hirota Koki, former premier and one-time ambassador to the USSR, even hinted that if the Soviet army and the Japanese navy would join forces, they could make East and South East Asia their own exclusive domain eliminating the Anglo-Saxon Powers, but the Soviet Union did not evince any interest in these offers.[33] Nevertheless Japan continued to pin her hopes on the USSR, as she feared that a direct approach to the Allies would bring merely a repetition of the unacceptable demand for unconditional surrender. She decided to send a special envoy to Moscow on behalf of the Emperor to explain Japan's proposals for peace.[34] But the whole episode seeking Soviet mediation turned out to be angling in water where no fish lived.

The USSR thus missed an opportunity given by Japan for increasing her influence over Japan and improving her image among the Japanese people. Her refusal to mediate on behalf of Japan might have been forgiven, but her last minute attack on Japan was considered a stab in the back and left a lasting bitterness in the minds of the Japanese people. This brought into focus the Soviet objective that she wanted a Japan completely crushed. While honouring her commitment to the United States to enter the Pacific War, the Soviet Union also hoped to participate in the occupation of Japan. But the atom bombs ended the war before a single Russian soldier could set

---

directive from the Emperor declared that the hostilities should be ended through the good offices of the USSR. See Robert J. C. Butow, *Japan's Decision to Surrender* (Stanford, 1954), pp. 88–89.

33. *Shusen shiroku,* pp. 348–49, 421–24.

34. Cable to Ambassador Sato Naotake in the Soviet Union, in *Potsdam Papers,* vol. 1, p. 879.

foot in Japan. President Truman refused to let the USSR occupy Hokkaido. He was willing to allow the dispatch of a token Soviet force under the overall command of General Douglas MacArthur, who had been appointed Supreme Commander of the Allied Powers, but this the Soviet Union did not accept. Her brief participation in the war had sufficed, however, for her to occupy South Sakhalin and the Kuriles and thus to take what she had been promised at Yalta.

Although Japan had solicited Soviet help at a moment of desperation, her distrust of the USSR and of Communist subversion remained undiminished. Her proposal for a joint Soviet-Japanese effort to drive the Anglo-Saxon Powers out of East Asia and South East Asia had been rejected. But Japan did not expect the wartime cooperation between the United States and the USSR to continue and planned to exploit the confrontation that would ensue.

The American State Department envisioned a postwar world in which Japan would not be a great power. Stability in the Far East would be maintained by China, aided by the United States. But while most State Department planners thought in terms of the enforcement of peace by an international organization,[35] Secretary of the Navy James V. Forrestal posed the question whether the United States should seek to make China or Japan into a counterweight to Russian influence.[36] Secretary of War Henry L. Stimson had proposed the deletion of Kyoto from the list of targets for the atomic bomb lest the bitterness aroused by the destruction of the sacred city prevent the wooing of Japan in the event of aggression in Man-

35. *Yalta Papers*, pp. 351–7.
36. Walter Millis, ed., *The Forrestal Diaries* (New York, 1958), pp. 52–53, 55–56.

churia. Truman seems to have agreed with Stimson.[37] Thus although Herbert Feis states that "even when final victory was near, the Soviet Union and the United States had not dealt with one another as rival claimants or antagonists for the right to occupy or control Japan after the war,"[38] the President and the War and Navy Secretaries had started thinking before Japan surrendered about American influence in Japan gaining ascendency over that of the Soviet Union.

The American determination that the United States should play a dominant role in the occupation of Japan and that there be but one occupation zone spared Japan the pain and misery of division, experienced by Germany and Korea. Thus Soviet-American rivalry proved advantageous to Japan even before the occupation began. General Anami was right in his calculation that it would not be in the interests of the USSR to have a weakened Japan in her future confrontation with the United States—that Japan had the capability of assisting one power against the other—but the power which was in a position to exploit Japan for her own purpose after the war was the United States and not the USSR. In her desire to "break Japan's spine" the Soviet Union had been blind to the postwar power configuration in the Far East and to the potentiality of Japan.

37. *Potsdam Papers,* vol. 2, p. 1373, footnote 3.
38. Herbert Feis, *Contest over Japan* (New York, 1967), p. 6.

1

Surrender and Occupation

Allied Control Machinery

Fear that the landing of Soviet forces in Japan would contribute to the spread of Communism among the disillusioned populace induced the Japanese government to surrender to the Allies as soon as the USSR invaded Manchuria.[1] Severe as an American occupation might be, it figured correctly that the United States would remain anti-Communist in spite of her wartime collaboration with the USSR and would not let Japan fall prey to Communism. While Japan played no positive role in the settlement of the terms for the surrender and the occupation of Japan, the United States herself reduced Soviet

1. Seisaburo Shinobu, *Sengo Nihon seiji shi 1945–52* (Tokyo, 1965), vol. 1, pp. 108–109; Rodger Swearingen and Paul Langer, *Red Flag in Japan* (Harvard, 1952), p. 87; Japan, Home Ministry, Police Bureau, Security Section "Kakushu joho narabini minshin no doko," Selected Archives of the Japanese Army, Navy and other Government Agencies 1868–1945, microfilm T 1490 (R220F90895); "Tokuyo sonota sayoku bunshi dosei toji," microfilm T 1492 (R220F-91748).

influence in Japanese affairs to a minimum. Her rejection of the Soviet request for the occupation of Hokkaido prevented a north-south division of Japan, and won the United States a good deal of favour in Japan.[2]

However, on 5 June 1945, the President had approved a recommendation by the State-War-Navy Co-ordinating Committee (SWNCC) for the formation of a Far Eastern Advisory Commission (FEAC) on the lines of the European Advisory Commission, composed of the Allied nations which had actively participated in the war against Japan.[3]

On 21 August 1945, the proposal for the FEAC was submitted to the United Kingdom, China and the USSR, with France, the Philippines, Australia, Canada, New Zealand and the Netherlands also being invited to participate in the commission. The FEAC, with its headquarters at Washington, was to make policy recommendations for the occupation of Japan in accordance with the principles laid down in the instrument of surrender.

Although the proposal did not mention the method of voting within the FEAC, the United States had held all along that she should have controlling authority. The national composition of the occupation forces, approved by Truman on 18 August 1945, had indicated American predominance. The decisive position of the United States had been envisaged also in the document on "United States Initial Post-Surrender Policy."[4]

2. Shigeru Yoshida, *The Yoshida Memoirs: The Story of Japan in Crisis* (London, 1961), p. 53.

3. George Blakeslee, *The Far Eastern Commission: A Study in International Co-operation* (Washington, 1953), pp. 2–3.

4. Supreme Commander for the Allied Powers, *Political Reorientation of Japan September 1945 to September 1948,* hereafter cited as *Political Reorientation of Japan,* (Washington, 1949), vol. 2, pp. 423–26.

Surprisingly, the USSR and China agreed to the proposal for the establishment of the FEAC; it was the United Kingdom which demanded the formation also of a Control Council, as the commission would have only advisory powers. The United Kingdom later waived her objection, but by then the Soviet Union had changed her mind. At the Conference of Foreign Ministers in London in September 1945, though Japan was not on the agenda, Vyacheslav Molotov read out a statement outlining the Russian proposal for an Allied Control Council of the Four Powers, which would "define and formulate the policies of the Allies towards Japan." He followed this up with a letter to Secretary of State James F. Byrnes stating that it would be wise to have an advisory commission composed of more than four major powers under the chairmanship of the United States, but that the Soviet Union could not agree to the proposal unless a Control Council were also created.[5] In other words, the Soviet Union desired to share with the United States responsibility for both the formulation and execution of occupation policies.[6] However, since the proposal for the FEAC had been accepted in principle, Byrnes suggested that this commission should meet and discuss the need for a Control Council.

The FEAC held its meetings at Washington from 30 October 1945 to 21 December 1945; they were attended by all members except the Soviet Union. These sessions were mainly ceremonial. On 26 December 1945, the American representative on the commission, General

5. George Blakeslee, "Negotiating to Establish the Far Eastern Commission, 1945" in Raymond Dennett, ed., *Negotiating with the Russians* (Boston, 1951), pp. 121–22; J. F. Byrnes, *Speaking Frankly* (London, 1947), pp. 213–18.
6. Blakeslee, "Negotiating," p. 122.

Frank R. McCoy, left for Japan with the FEAC policy paper "Post Surrender Policy for Japan," which followed closely the "United States Initial Post-Surrender Policy."[7] In the meantime, correspondence continued between the United States and the USSR on the question of the Control Council. The Soviet government voiced its fears that the unilateral policies of the United States might result in a Japan antagonistic to the USSR. Considering the fact that Japan had been a constant menace to Russian security for the past two decades, the Soviet desire to be free from a renewed threat was justifiable.[8] But the United States stuck firmly to her decision that neither the American government nor General MacArthur would allow themselves to be divested of the responsibility for making and enforcing final decisions. At the Moscow Conference, which lasted from 16 December to 27 December, 1945, a compromise was worked out. It was agreed to set up an eleven power Far Eastern Commission (FEC) with headquarters at Washington and a four power Allied Council for Japan (ACJ) to sit in Tokyo and consult with and advise the Supreme Commander, Allied Powers (SCAP), who, however, would retain controlling authority. The United States obtained assent to the supremacy of SCAP in Japan by citing the powers of the Soviet chairmen of the Allied Control Commissions in Rumania, Bulgaria and Hungary, where the provision that the British and American representatives should be consulted was not always strictly interpreted and the Soviet chairmen's actions were not fettered in any way. The power of veto

7. Blakeslee, *Far Eastern Commission,* p. 9. The clause that "in the event of any differences of opinion among them [the Allies], the policies of US will govern," had been omitted in the "Post-Surrender Policy for Japan," but this did not signal a change in American intentions.

8. Blakeslee, "Negotiating," p. 127.

was accepted in return for the right of the United States to issue interim directives, subject to review by the commission, on the ground that where there was a deadlock due to disagreement among the members, there must be an alternative to keep the occupation machinery running smoothly. The United States conceded that no fundamental changes in the Japanese constitutional structure or in the regime of the Occupation would be made without prior consultation with and consent of the commission.[9]

Analyzing the struggle of the United States and the USSR over the control machinery of Japan, it may be concluded that though the United States modified her original insistence on unilateral formulation of policies governing Japan, she did not fully grant the Soviet Union's demand for participation in the formulation and execution of these policies. The USSR obtained the right to discuss policies in the commission and to veto policies of which she disapproved. At the same time, America's power to issue interim directives and cast a veto of her own, prevented the formulation of any policies not acceptable to the United States. Although the Soviet Union's demand for an Allied Council was accepted, the endowment of the Supreme Commander with sole executive authority left little scope for placing restrictions on him by any country other than the United States. In short, the Soviet Union succeeded in getting two organs, which could be used by her as sounding boards for her opinions, but which

9. *Ibid.*, pp. 130–34; *Political Reorientation of Japan*, vol. 2, pp. 421–2. The members of the Far Eastern Commission were the USA, the USSR, the UK, France, China, the Netherlands, Canada, Australia, New Zealand, India and the Philippines. The members of the Allied Council for Japan were the USA, the USSR, China and a member jointly representing the UK, Australia, New Zealand and India.

held little guarantee that the Japan that was being rebuilt would not be inimical to her. Yet while the channels of control were closed to her, the Soviet Union obtained the privilege of observing the process of reshaping Japan closely, on the spot. Her direct contacts with the Japanese people kept open the possibility of achieving some degree of success in her efforts to mould a Japan friendly with the Soviet Union.

The Soviet Union and the Japan Communist Party

SCAP unwittingly helped the Soviet Union to establish easy contacts with the Japanese people by legalizing the Communist Party for the first time in Japanese history. Ever haunted by the fear of Communist revolution, the Japanese government had not relaxed its wartime censorship or arrest of Communists even after its acceptance of the surrender terms. But the SCAP directive of 4 October 1945 suspended all decrees and laws restricting freedom of thought and speech, and all the latent revolutionary forces were revived.[10] The released leaders of the Communist Party, having fought consistently against Japanese militarism, could effectively disclaim any responsibility for the war and present themselves as true champions of democracy.[11]

Postwar Japan presented ideal conditions for the revival of the Communist movement. The devastation of the country and the disintegration of her economy, the hunger of the people and, above all, their disillusionment

10. Japan, Ministry of Foreign Affairs, *Documents Concerning the Allied Occupation and Control of Japan* (Tokyo, 1951), vol. 2, pp. 82–86.

11. *Rodo Kumiai* editorial, dated 19 April 1947, in Nikkan Rodo Tsushin Sha, *Rodo kumiai no shido wo nerau Nihon kyosanto*, hereafter *Rodo kumiai*, (Tokyo, 1954), p. 18.

in the ideals and values of "invincible Japan" left Japan susceptible to the spread of an ideology which appealed to the downtrodden and which had predicted the collapse of Japanese imperialism. Many intellectuals had been drawn to Marxism since the beginning of the twentieth century. Fear of persecution had forced them to conceal their "dangerous thoughts." With the proclamation of freedom of thought and expression by the Occupation authorities they could propagate their Marxist beliefs with new conviction. The Communists were quick to take advantage of this situation and exploit the Occupation's zeal to revive and strengthen democratic trends in the country.

The Occupation encouraged the Communists in the belief that all democratic forces, be they even Communist, would provide a counterweight to ultrarightist movements, that might be gathering strength underground. Though no such movements materialized, the fears of the Occupation authorities were not unreasonable, considering the high pitch to which nationalist feelings had been aroused during the war.

The Occupation's zeal for a free press and for the revival and development of labour unions facilitated Communist action. SCAP welcomed the participation of Communists in such important bodies as the Central and Local Labour Relations Commissions. Tokuda Kyuichi, who subsequently became secretary general of the Communist Party, was one of the members of the Commission for Labour Legislation (*Romu Hosei Shingi Kai*) set up by the government on 27 October 1945 for drafting trade union laws.[12] Meanwhile the Communist Party hailed the Occupation forces as liberators and identified itself with

12. Iwao Ayusawa, *A History of Labour in Modern Japan* (Honolulu, 1966), pp. 250–51.

the objectives of the Occupation.[13] It showed unexpected restraint and spoke often convincingly of achieving social justice and of building a democratic Japan through a process of peaceful revolution. Nozaka Sanzo, who had fled to the Soviet Union and China during the 1930's and was included upon his return after the war in the Central Executive Committee of the Communist Party, openly stressed that the party should be made into a "lovable party" and should become a People's Party.[14] At the Fifth Convention, held in February 1946, the party resolved to work for the establishment of a democratic people's government by carrying out a bourgeois democratic revolution and only after reaching that stage would it take the next step to a socialist revolution. It emphasized that peaceful democratic means would be employed in carrying out this revolution.[15]

MacArthur's policy of not interfering in Japanese affairs directly, unless security was endangered, facilitated Communist activity. The Communist organ *Akahata* was issued within ten days of the release of the Communist leaders, who toured the country to enlist support for the establishment of a "democratic people's government."

Since the Labour Unions were "training schools for carrying out class struggles," the Communists attempted to take over their leadership. The Action Policy passed at the Fourth Convention, held in December 1945, had

13. Resolution passed by the Annual Convention of JCP on 1 December, 1945, see Nihon Hyoron Sha, *Shiryo: Sengo niju nen shi, Seiji* (Tokyo, 1966), pp. 405–406.

14. Nozaka's address at a public meeting in Hibiya Park on 26 January, 1946, *see* Nihon Kyosanto Chuo Iinkai, Sanzo Nozaka, *Sansenshu sengo hen, 1946 January–1961 February* (Tokyo, 1966), pp. 13–19. Rekishi Gakukenkyukai, *Sengo Nihon shi* (Tokyo, 1961), vol. 1, p. 89.

15. *Rodo Kumiai*, pp. 78–79.

made clear the party's target of establishing one trade union in every industry. MacArthur's directive of 11 October 1945 to Premier Shidehara Kijuro demanding, among other things, the encouragement of unionization of labour and the abolition of all repressive laws including police control in spheres of industrial relations gave a great impetus to the reorganization of trade unions. By December 1945, labour unions had increased from zero to 509, with a membership of 380,677, and the number continued to increase at a rate unparalleled in Japanese history.[16] The Trade Union Act, promulgated in December 1945 and put into effect in March 1946, guaranteed the rights of organization and collective bargaining to all wage earning workers, including public servants with the exception of policemen, jailors and firemen, and made illegal discrimination by employers on grounds of organization of trade unions or engaging in union activities.

Beginning with the reorganization of the Seamen's Union by prewar veterans, labour unions sprang up separately in all enterprises led by the leaders of the old *Sodomei*.[17] The *Sodomei* itself was reorganized on 1 August 1946. In response to an appeal made by the Communist Party, leftist leaders met on 5 December 1945 and again on 6 January 1946 to form the Kanto Regional Council. With the employees of newspaper, communication and broadcasting agencies as the core, a new organization, the *Nippon Sangyo Betsu Rodo Kumiai Kaigi* (*Sanbetsu*), was established on 14 August 1946 with a membership of 1,574,000. While the *Sodomei* consisted of craft unions, the *Sanbetsu* was a federation of industry

16. Ayusawa, pp. 257–58.
17. The *Dai Nippon Rodo Sodomei Yuaikai*, started in 1912 by Suzuki Bunji.

unions.[18] Out of the nineteen members of the executive committee of *Sanbetsu,* thirteen were Communists; out of the total forty-three members of the Action Committee, thirty were Communists. It should be noted also that many of the labour unions in government enterprises, such as the Railway Workers Union and the Communication Workers Union, were led by Communists.[19] Although the *Sodomei* turned down a proposal by the *Sanbetsu* to form a national united front, the initial success of the Communists in taking over the leadership of labour unions was striking.

The Communist leaders incited the workers to direct action. Forced to labour for long hours at low wages and suffering from rising prices and a shortage of food, the workers eagerly accepted Communist leadership. They seized the management of factories and produced and delivered goods or performed services without giving the owners a voice in management. The *Asahi Shimbun* and *Yomiuri Shimbun,* newspapers with a very large circulation, were seized by the employees and "democratized" by October 1945.[20] The seizure of control of industries became one of the tactics used by the labour unions for "democratization" and the satisfaction of their demands.

The success of labour unions in realizing their major demands, including union recognition, collective bargaining, shorter working hours, and longer vacations with pay, immediately after the war was due not only to the strength of the labour movement or the effectiveness of its leadership but also to the state of stupor (*kyodatsu jotai*) into which the employers seemed to have fallen.

18. Ayusawa, pp. 257–58.
19. *Rodo Kumiai,* pp. 23–25.
20. *Sengo Nihon shi,* p. 97.

When the tactic of production control (*seisan kanri*) spread to government and municipal offices in Tokyo, however, the government on 13 June 1946 ruled production control as illegal and warned that the sabotage of production would be punished severely.[21]

Apart from the new tactic of seizing control of management, the unions used the time-honoured weapon of strikes, taking advantage of the fact that the Occupation authorities were more sympathetic toward the workers than toward industrialists and government officials. As the economic hardships increased and the food crisis worsened, the Communist Party played up the difficulties of the people and organized a series of demonstrations, which reached their climax in the May Day demonstrations and food riots, reminiscent of the rice riots of 1918. MacArthur's warning on 20 May 1946 that if such violent activities continued, he would be forced to take steps to put an end to them was ignored by the Communist Party, which staged the so-called October Offensive on the part of the electrical workers, who clamored for a wage increase, repeal of the income tax on salaries, and removal of limits set on wages paid in cash. Meanwhile civil servants of various government departments asked for higher wages and, forming an All Government Municipal Employees United Struggle Committee, threatened to stage a nation-wide strike if their demands were not met.[22]

The concessions gained by the above workers, the relative success of other direct action, the lenient, non-interfering attitude of SCAP and the provision in Article 6 of the Principles for Japanese Trade Unions, adopted

21. Ayusawa, pp. 259–62; *Rodo Kumiai*, p. 21.
22. Nihon Hyoron Sha, *Shiryo sengo niju nen shi: Rodo* (Tokyo, 1966), pp. 7–11.

by the FEC, allowing the trade unions to take part in political activities and to support political parties encouraged the Communists to entertain the naive idea that if they staged a general strike and succeeded in overthrowing the government, SCAP would give its blessing to this change of government through the "freely expressed will of the people of Japan."[23] But the general strike, set for 1 February 1947, never materialized. When the leaders of the Joint Struggle Committee did not heed an informal request by SCAP to call off the strike, MacArthur formally forbade the strike, and the Communist Party complied with his order.[24]

The failure of the Communist Party to stage the strike impaired its prestige and popularity. Although it put up 120 candidates for the House of Representatives in the general election of April 1947, only 4 were elected. Another 4 were elected to the House of Councillors, though 40 had stood for office.

Even within the *Sanbetsu,* criticism was mounting against the Communist leaders, and in February 1948, a split occurred with the birth of the *Sanbetsu Minshuka Domei.*[25] Started with the initiative and encouragement of SCAP, the new *Mindo* movement gained strength rapidly and became an efficient counterbalance to the Communist labour organization.[26]

SCAP also thwarted a major strike called by the railway and communication workers in March 1948 and

23. For the FEC policy decision on trade unions, *see* United States, Department of State, *Activities of Far Eastern Commission, February 26, 1946–10 July, 1947* (Washington, 1947), pp. 26–27 and 91–92.

24. *Shiryo Rodo,* pp. 49–51. Ayusawa, pp. 270–72.

25. *Rodo Kumiai,* pp. 29–31.

26. Ayusawa, pp. 287–89; SCAP, General Headquarters, *Summation of Non-military Activities,* February 1948.

averted the July offensive of organized labour by imposing increasing restraints on its freedom of action. MacArthur suggested that the right of collective bargaining by public servants be restricted, lest a strike by them paralyze the government they had sworn to support.[27] The stiffening attitude of SCAP toward organized labour and its declining hostility toward the men who had been "most active in building up and running the war machine,"[28] were reflected in the enactment by the Diet in December 1948 of the Japanese National Railways Act, the Japanese Monopoly Public Corporation Act and the Public Corporation and National Enterprises Labour Relations Act, which removed the national public servants (the white collar workers, of the central government) and the blue collar workers engaged in the various enterprises of the government (organized henceforth into "public corporations" or "public enterprises") from the jurisdiction of the Central Labour Relations Commission. This weakened the labour movement, since it separated the large body of public workers who occupied the commanding position in the movement from the workers of private industries and deprived one third of Japan's unions and about the same proportion of organized workers of the right to strike.[29]

The Communist Party, whose prestige had already been affected by its failure to bring off the general strike in February 1947, now lost greatly in popularity, for the restrictions imposed on the workers by the government were attributed to the violent policies of the Communist

27. *Shiryo Rodo,* pp. 95–97; *Political Reorientation of Japan,* vol. 2, pp. 581–83.

28. Secretary of the Army Kenneth C. Royall's speech in *Documents Concerning the Allied Occupation and Control of Japan,* vol. 2, pp. 4–10; Macmohan Ball, *Japan Enemy or Ally* (New York, 1949), pp. 129–30.

29. *Shiryo Rodo,* p. 108; Ayusawa, pp. 293–94.

leaders, who seemed motivated by their political plans of carrying out a "peaceful revolution." Not only had the Communist leadership failed to increase the influence of the workers, it had lost the rights they had been granted at the beginning of the Occupation.

Other blunders by the Japanese Communist Party affected not only its own popularity but that of the Soviet Union. Nozaka's declaration that the Communist Party should become a "lovable party" and Secretary-General Tokuda's repeated denials that the party had any ties with the Soviet Union had marked a change in the tactics of the Japanese Communist Party from prewar days. But though it reduced its material ties with the Soviet Union, there is every reason to believe that their basic relationship remained unchanged.[30]

The Soviet mission in Japan had a staff of 500, compared with the 334 persons of the other 16 foreign missions combined. The Soviet personnel was reduced to 312 in 1947 only after repeated protests by SCAP. Although it is difficult to assess the physical assistance given by the Soviet mission to the Japanese Communist Party,[31] later events clearly showed that the Party's ties with the USSR had never been broken and that it acted under the direction of the Soviet Union.

In deemphasizing the question of the retention of the Emperor in the period from 1945 to 1950 in deference to the wishes of the vast majority of the Japanese people,

---

30. Swearingen and Langer, *Red Flag in Japan,* pp. 134–35 and 230–31; Langer and Swearingen, "The Japanese Communist Party, the Soviet Union and Korea," *Pacific Affairs* vol. 23, December 1950, p. 345.

31. David J. Dallin, *Soviet Russia and the Far East* (London, 1949), pp. 268–69; Harry Emerson Wildes, *Typhoon in Tokyo: The Occupation and its Aftermath* (New York, 1954), p. 280.

the Communist Party echoed Soviet policy.[32] When in 1950 it became vociferous in its clamor for the abolition of the Emperor system, it again followed the initiative of Moscow, which had revived its demand that the Emperor should be tried as a war criminal.[33]

The ties of the Communist Party with the USSR were made clear on the question of the repatriation of Japanese prisoners. While the repatriation of Japanese residents from other regions was completed by the end of 1946, the return of Japanese nationals from Siberia and other Russian territories was not begun until 19 December 1946. Although the United States had objected to Soviet use of Japanese prisoners for the reconstruction of war-devastated areas as contrary to the Potsdam Declaration which provided for their speedy repatriation,[34] the Soviet authorities used the prisoners in reconstruction work, and their return proceeded at a snail's pace in spite of sharp protests from the SCAP in the Allied Council for Japan.[35] Suspending repatriation for months ostensibly for climatic reasons, the Soviets used the delay to indoctrinate the prisoners in order to reinforce the Communist Party in Japan.[36] In spite of public denials, the Japanese

32. For the views of the Japanese Communist Party on the Emperor system, see Nozaka, pp. 11–12. Shinobu, vol. 1, p. 250; Swearingen, p. 135; *Akahata*, 11 July 1948. The results of public opinion polls published in *Asahi* in December 1945 show that only 5% wanted the Emperor system abolished; 75% wanted it reformed and retained.

33. *Akahata*, 3, 5, 7, 6 February 1950; *New Times* (Moscow) 1 March 1950, pp. 21–22, 15 March 1950, pp. 26–27; 1 May 1950, pp. 26–27.

34. Byrnes, p. 243; Dallin, pp. 240, 270–74.

35. Dallin, p. 274; *Nippon Times*, 21 December 1946.

36. *Tokyo*, 14 May 1949; Nisso Shinzen Kyokai, *Soren wa Nihon ni nani wo nozumu ka* (Tokyo, 1949), pp. 92–97; *Corrected Verbatim Minutes of the Allied Council for Japan*, Meeting on 29 October 1947.

Communist Party seems to have established liaison with the Russian repatriation agencies[37] and was alleged to have specifically requested the Russian repatriation agencies not to return the Japanese prisoners without first indoctrinating them.[38] Whether or not the Japanese Communist Party had made such a plea, there can be no doubt about the indoctrination of the prisoners, who came back shouting slogans against American imperialism and monopoly capitalism and, ignoring their anxiously waiting families, hastened to the local Communist headquarters to pay their homage. Had the indoctrinated repatriates quietly fanned through the country, their propaganda might have been effective, but their behaviour alienated the people not only from Communism but from the Soviet Union.[39] Soviet radio broadcasts from Vladivostok, Khabarovsk and Moscow to the effect that the USSR was the only country genuinely desirous of peace and that the Japanese people should rally to the support of the Communist Party also were counterproductive.[40]

Nozaka's abandonment of the "lovable party" concept in favor of a more radical approach at the behest of the Cominform and the decision of the Eighteenth Convention of the Central Executive Committee no longer to limit the objectives of the party to the domestic question of overthrowing the Yoshida Cabinet, but to propagate anti-Americanism and anti-imperialism,[41] aroused public indignation, especially when a series of strikes and mount-

37. *Akahata,* 2–3 March 1950; *Tokyo,* 3 March 1950.

38. *Pravda,* on 5 March 1950, as quoted in *Current Digest of the Soviet Press,* hereafter CDSP, vol. 2, no. 11, p. 22; *Asahi,* 26 March 1950; *Mainichi,* 27 March 1950.

39. Wildes, p. 283.

40. Swearingen and Langer, *Red Flag in Japan,* p. 233; Stalin's New Year message to the Japanese people, *Shiryo Seiji,* p. 656.

41. *Akahata,* 24 January 1950.

ing violence were taken as the result of the new policy,[42] whether or not the Communists had actually been responsible in all instances.[43] The government took advantage of this threat to law and order to ram through the Diet the Subversive Activities Prevention Bill.[44]

The change in Soviet strategy may be attributed in part to the realization that while the soft line adopted by the Japanese Communist Party had yielded some initial results, the "old guard" had not been dislodged, in fact it was more firmly entrenched, and the possibility of a "peaceful revolution" was remote. The establishment of the Chinese People's Republic in 1949 had no doubt contributed to the shift toward belligerence as had the military offensive that was about to be launched in Korea.

The Soviet Union and the Japanese Communist Party overplayed their hand. The forceful resistence of the Communist-dominated unions to the government's personnel retrenchment programme in early 1949, caused disaffection among workers, so that by June 1950 the *Sanbetsu* had dwindled to slightly more than one quarter of its former membership and with MacArthur's directive purging Communists, lost the opportunity of rebuilding its ranks.[45]

Lulled into a false sense of security by the breeze of freedom that had blown in the early years of the Occupa-

42. Editorials in *Yomiuri*, 28 July 1950; *Jiji*, 30 August 1950 and 25 September 1950; *Tokyo*, 11 June 1950; *Asahi*, 18 June 1950.

43. *Shiryo Seiji*, pp. 71–73; *Shiryo Rodo*, pp. 127–34; *Rodo Kumiai*, p. 33.

44. *Ayusawa*, pp. 322–3; *Shiryo Rodo*, p. 192.

45. *Asahi*, 7 and 24 June 1950; 24 July 1950. Editorials in *Yomiuri*, 12 May 1950, 7 June 1950, 28 July 1950; *Tokyo*, 11 June 1950; *Jiji*, 30 August 1950, 27 September 1950; *Nihon Keizai*, 2 September 1950.

tion, the Communists had not appreciated the fact that MacArthur would not allow Japan to go Communist and would bear down heavily on the Communist Party when he perceived the danger of total subversion. The failure of the Communist Party to win the support of the Japanese public was paralleled by the inability of the USSR to better her image in Japan.[46]

The Soviet Union in the Far Eastern Commission and the Allied Council for Japan

Soviet policy toward Japan was not confined, of course, to support of the Communist Party. As mentioned already, the USSR was represented on the Far Eastern Commission and on the Allied Council for Japan. How successful was she in formulating policies, which were in her own national interest or in preventing the formulation of policies which ran counter to them?

According to the Agreement evolved at the Moscow Conference, the United States Government could issue interim directives to the Supreme Commander pending action by the Commission whenever urgent matters arose not covered by policies already formulated by the Commission, "provided that any directives dealing with *fundamental changes in the Japanese constitutional structure or in the regime of control* or dealing with a change in the Japanese Government as a whole will be issued only following consultation and following the attainment of agreement in the Far Eastern Commission."[47]

46. Yoshida, p. 228; Allan B. Cole and Naomichi Nakanishi (comp. and ed.), *Japanese Opinion Polls with Socio-Political Significance 1947–1957* (Ann Arbor, 1959), pp. 3, 5, 8, 10, 11, 21–24, 27, 30, 33, 36–37, 56, 61, 63, 65, 80, 648–49.

47. *Political Reorientation of Japan*, vol. 2, p. 421. Emphasis added.

The Soviet Union had reason to expect, therefore, that no fundamental change in the Japanese government would be carried out without her wishes being considered. But MacArthur drafted a new Constitution without consulting or informing even his own government, presenting it with a *fait accompli* for its approval.

MacArthur disagreed with the principle of limiting America's unilateral authority over Japan and of controlling his activity by the formation of two unwieldy international bodies.[48] He failed to prevent the establishment of the FEC and the ACJ, but proceeded to ignore their wishes. To preclude interference by the FEC once it came into being officially the new constitution was drafted within six days.[49] While the SWNCC had stipulated on 11 January 1946 that "only as a last resort should a formal instruction be issued to the Japanese Government specifying in detail the reforms to be effected," leaving open the question whether the Imperial institution would be retained or not and making no provision for the renunciation of war,[50] MacArthur pressured the Japanese Cabinet into accepting and speedily implementing his draft, by warning that if it delayed, the FEC might come up with a constitution that would abolish the monarchy.[51] MacArthur's arguments were given weight by the Soviet Union's demand that the

48. *Ibid.,* p. 744; Courtney Whitney, *MacArthur, his Rendezvous with History* (New York, 1956), pp. 298–9; Theodore McNelly, "The Japanese Constitution: Child of the Cold War," *Political Science Quarterly,* vol. 74, June 1959, pp. 182–83.

49. *Political Reorientation of Japan,* vol. 2, pp. 622–23; McNelly, p. 184; Whitney, p. 247; Robert E. Ward, "The Origins of the Present Japanese Constitution", *The American Political Science Review,* vol. 50, December 1956, pp. 992–93.

50. McNelly, pp. 178–180; Ward, pp. 989–91, footnote 23.

51. McNelly, pp. 187–8. Toshio Sugimoto, *Senryo hiroku* (Tokyo, 1965), pp. 97, 101–103.

Emperor be tried as a war criminal and by the Japanese
Communist Party's call for the abolition of the imperial
institution. It was known also that Austrailia and the
Republic of China favored a republican form of government for Japan.[52]

The Soviet objective of abolishing the monarchy and
curtailing the "old guard", while increasing the influence
of the workers, was defeated by the *fait accompli* of an
"idealized version of Anglo-American political institutions hastily patched together." The constitution was a
weapon for defeating Russian intrigues in occupied
Japan. As Professor Theodore McNelly has pointed out,
ever since Perry's visit international politics rather than
domestic development had been instrumental in the
development of Japan's legal and political institutions.
The new constitution was a "child of the Cold War," an
"accouchement forcé."

The State Department and the FEC first learnt of the
new constitution when it was published in the Tokyo
press on 6 March 1946. Indignant, the FEC entertained
a resolution requiring MacArthur to submit the constitution for its approval and to postpone the elections, but
faced with the threat of an American veto, the commission modified its stand and merely asked to be kept
informed of the progress of the draft in the Japanese
Parliament and to be given an opportunity to approve
the final draft. The FEC did discuss the constitution and
agree on certain basic principles, basically the same as
those contained in the directives given by the State Department to MacArthur.

The Soviet representative's demand that the constitution be amended to provide for a unicameral legislature,
an elected judiciary, and social welfare measures failed

52. Ward, pp. 996–99.

to meet approval. Nor did his colleagues heed his com-
plaint when they passed a resolution to the effect that
the new constitution should be submitted to the people
after two to three years for a review, that the essential
question was not a review of the provisions of the constitution, but the fact that even "the few democratic
provisions which were contained in it were being sys-
tematically violated by US Occupation authorities and the
Japanese Government."[53] The Soviet Union was unsuccessful also in its efforts to achieve a postponement of
the elections on the ground that the democratic forces
needed more time to gather strength and that early elections would return the "old guard" to power. The FEC
actually asked SCAP to consider the advisability of post-
poning the elections, but MacArthur refused to accede to
the request.[54]

On the labour front, the FEC on 16 December 1946
unanimously passed a resolution incorporating principles
for a Japanese Trade Union Law.[55] The Labour Union
Law of December 1945 had provided for collective
bargaining and the right to strike. When the Labour Relations Adjustments Law restricting the right of government and public utility workers to strike had been proposed on 10 July 1946, the Soviet representative on the
Allied Council had objected and had vainly tried to sub-

53. Blakeslee, pp. 55, 65; *Activities of the Far Eastern Commission,* pp. 63–68; Hugh Borton, *Japan's Modern Century* (New York,
1955), pp. 403–405 and note 27; Hugh Borton, "Preparation for
the Occupation of Japan", *Journal of Asian Studies,* vol. 25, February,
1966, pp. 209–10; Ward, pp. 1006–1008.

54. Blakeslee, pp. 34–35; *Activities of the Far Eastern Commis-
mission,* pp. 11–16, 58–63; Soviet representative's speech in the ACJ
asking for the postponement of elections in *Soren wa Nihon ni nani
wo nozomu ka,* p. 9.

55. *Activities of the Far Eastern Commission,* pp. 91–93. Blakeslee,
pp. 170–75.

stitute a twenty-one point programme guaranteeing the workers' freedom to strike and control production.[56] In the face of mounting strike threats and violence, the government revised the labour laws under MacArthur's direction, denying collective bargaining and the right to strike to government workers; the employees of public corporations retained the right of collective bargaining but were forbidden to strike. The Soviet representative on the FEC had made a spate of protests against the new legislation and had demanded its abrogation on the ground that it contravened the FEC policy decision, which made no distinction between private and public employees. Australia and some of the other states had sympathized with the Soviet position, but did not try to block the new restrictions which MacArthur regarded as necessary, for such action would have embarrassed the United States government and forced it to use its veto power.[57]

On the fisheries question, the USSR also disagreed with MacArthur's recommendations concerning Japan's freedom of fishing and whaling. She insisted that Japanese fishing areas could be extended only with the prior authorization of the FEC. Yet SCAP ignored the FEC and extended the fishing areas at its discretion. It also authorized SCAP controlled whaling expeditions.[58] Soviet objections

56. Ball, pp. 156–7; *Nippon Times*, 14, 15, 17, July 1946; E. M. Martin, *Allied Occupation of Japan* (New York, 1948), pp. 84–85; *Soren wa Nihon ni nani wo nozomu ka*, pp. 31–37.

57. Blakeslee, pp. 170–75; *Soren wa Nihon ni nani wo nozomu ka*, pp. 123–28; *Corrected Verbatim Minutes of the Allied Council for Japan*, Meeting of 28 August, 1948.

58. Japan, Ministry of Agriculture and Forestry, *SCAP's Memoranda Relating to Agricultural Policies of Japan* (Tokyo, 1949), pp. 119, 123, 126; Japan, Ministry of Agriculture and Forestry, *Collection of SCAP's Memoranda* (Tokyo, 1949), pp. 107–109.

to these measures antagonized public opinion in Japan.

The USSR, along with other members of the FEC, opposed an American proposal, made in April 1949, permitting Japan to participate in international conventions, meetings, consular arrangements and other bilateral or multilateral accords, which SCAP might consider in the interests of the Occupation. But SCAP once again ignored the objections and through interim directives permitted an increase in Japan's external activities, including full membership in the Universal Postal Union, the International Telecommunications Union and several other specialized agencies of the United Nations.[59]

One of the major differences between the USSR and the United States concerning Japan was on the question of reparations. The payment of reparations by Japan had been stipulated by the Potsdam Declaration, the United States Post Surrender Policy for Japan of 29 August 1945 and the FEC Basic Surrender Policy for Japan, passed on 19 June 1947.[60] When the Pauley Report on Reparations, as amended by the SWNCC, was submitted to the FEC, the FEC drafted a policy on Interim Reparations Removals, which was more favourable to Japan than that of the American government. Its resolution could not be implemented, however, until agreement was reached on the percentage of reparations to be allocated to the various countries.[61] The main obstacle to such agreement was the insistence of the USSR that the assets she had removed from Manchuria, the Kuriles and Sakhalin should be treated as war booty and not be taken into account

59. United States, Department of State, Far Eastern Commission, *Second Report by the Secretary-General, July 10, 1947–December 23, 1948,* pp. 22–23, 36–37; Blakeslee, pp. 78–80.

60. *Political Reorientation of Japan,* vol. 2, p. 425; *Activities of the Far Eastern Commission,* pp. 56–57.

61. Blakeslee, p. 125; Ball, pp. 98–102.

when working out the reparations percentage. She rejected a compromise proposal by the United States that all countries retain the Japanese assests held by them on 1 June 1946, but that the total amount of such assets, including the war booty held by them, be considered in determining the percentage of reparations. The matter of Japanese reparations to the USSR was not resolved. In fact, while an interim SCAP directive, issued on 3 April 1947, provided for advance transfer of some reparations to China, the Philippines, the Dutch East Indies, Burma and Malaysia,[62] they were discontinued on 12 May 1949 as the American policy toward Japan shifted from democratization to rehabilitation.[63]

During the first two years of the Occupation, SCAP had refrained from issuing directives for the economic stabilization of Japan, deeming this to be the responsibility of the Japanese government and believing that Japanese industry and foreign trade would revive of their own accord.[64] When the Japanese government failed to take the necessary measures in food collection, tax collection and coal production, SCAP was forced to assume direct control,[65] prodded by the fact that by 1947 the trade deficit borne by the United States totalled 300 million dollars. When neither the Ashida government nor its successor, the Yoshida government, dared to implement the austerity measures proposed by the Young Mission, which had been dispatched from the United States to work out a comprehensive economic stabiliza-

62. Blakeslee, pp. 129–50; *Documents Concerning Allied Occupation,* vol. 3, pp. 272–76.

63. Blakeslee, pp. 151–68; *Documents Concerning Allied Occupation,* vol. 3, pp. 294–300.

64. Ball, p. 102; Hugh Borton et al., *The Far East 1942–46* (London, 1955), p. 349.

65. *Ibid.*

tion programme, SCAP did so on its own authority in December 1948.[66] The Soviet representative on the FEC agreed with the need to revive Japan's peacetime industries, but suggested supervision by a multinational management board to ensure that no war industries be rebuilt.[67] But SCAP ignored the reservations of the USSR and other members of the FEC who had misgivings about a rejuvenated Japan and went ahead with its Economic Stabilization Programme.[68] Attempts by the Communist Party of Japan to arouse the public against it, contributed to MacArthur's decision to purge the Communists.

The Peace Treaty Issue

Believing that the official termination of the state of war would stimulate the economic recovery of Japan, MacArthur had recommended as early as March 1947 that a peace treaty with Japan be concluded as soon as possible.[69] When the United States, in view of the dead-

66. MacArthur's letter to Yoshida dated 19 December 1948, *Documents Concerning Allied Occupation,* vol. 3, pp. 26–28; *Rodo Kumiai,* p. 33.
67. Chugoku Sekai Chishiki Sha, *Nihon mondai bunken shu,* pp. 183–85.
68. Panyushkin's speech in the FEC condemning the unilateral actions of the USA to stabilize the Japanese economy, disregarding the Commission's directives, *Pravda,* 29 January 1949, as quoted in *CDSP,* vol. 1, no. 5, pp. 29–31; Panyushkin's criticism in the FEC against the grant of privileged conditions for American monopolies to invest in Japan, *Pravda,* 20 February 1949, *CDSP,* vol. 1, no. 7, pp. 27–28. *Izvestiya* claimed on 6 March 1949 that "the USA plans to utilize Japan as a sphere for investment of American capital and turn her into a dependent colony, while the Soviet Union aims to develop the Far Eastern countries through creation of national industries." (*CDSP,* vol. 1, no. 9, pp. 22–23; Also see *Akahata,* 6 June 1950.)
69. *Political Reorientation of Japan,* vol. 2, p. 765; F. C. Dunn, *Peacemaking and the Settlement with Japan* (Princeton, 1963), pp.

lock over Germany at the Foreign Ministers' Conference, on 11 July 1947 invited the other ten members of the FEC to discuss a peace treaty at a preliminary conference, at which a two-thirds majority vote would suffice for reaching decisions,[70] the USSR objected in her reply of 22 July 1947 that according to the Potsdam Conference preparations for a peace were to be made by the Council of Foreign Ministers, where the powers had a veto. To Secretary of State George C. Marshall's contention on 12 August that the formation of the FEC had constituted recognition of the primary interests of eleven powers in post-surrender policy matters and that the Council of Foreign Ministers was thus not representative enough for deliberation concerning a peace treaty, the Soviet Union retorted on 29 August that the Council of Foreign Ministers had been established for the preparation of a peace settlement in Asia as well as in Europe, as could be seen from the inclusion of a Chinese delegate.[71]

Secretary of State Byrnes had indeed urged at Potsdam the participation of China in the Council of Foreign Ministers to facilitate discussion of peace with Japan,[72] but now that she wanted to keep Japan on her side, the United States realized that the Council of Foreign Ministers with its unanimity principle would not be a convenient body for this purpose.

54–55. Borton points out that the State Department in early 1947 actually compiled the first draft of a peace treaty and informed MacArthur of its contents, but did not authorize him to make a public announcement of it. (Hugh Borton et al., *Far East*, p. 422.)

70. Dunn, pp. 62–66; United States, *Department of State Bulletin*, hereafter *DSB*, 27 July 1947, p. 182. While the Japanese press displayed interest in the early attempts at peace, *Yomiuri* warned that a separate peace treaty would worsen the Far Eastern situation. *Asahi*, 18 July 1947; *Yomiuri*, 15 July 1947.

71. *Documents 1947–48*, pp. 715–20.

72. *Potsdam Papers*, vol. 1, p. 67.

China objected to the mode of voting proposed by the United States and sided with the USSR in demanding veto power. Her reluctance to participate in a peace conference from which the Soviet Union abstained, may have been due to the fear that this might be construed as a violation of the Sino-Soviet Agreement of 1945, forbidding a separate peace with Japan, and might serve as an excuse for Soviet aid to the Chinese Communists.[73] As Great Britain and the Commwealth countries did not share MacArthur's optimism that Japan had been converted to pacificism and democracy and dreaded the ruinous competition that an unchecked Japanese economic recovery could bring,[74] the proposed conference never materialized. The delay was to Japan's advantage, as the restrictive punitive measures of the early draft were discarded by the United States with the intensification of the Cold War, lest the USSR and the Chinese People's Republic lure Japan into their orbit by offering more attractive peace terms.[75]

Although Soviet efforts to gain influence in Japan through the Communist Party had been foiled during the Occupation by direct and indirect countermeasures on the part of SCAP as well as by the mistakes of the party, there was reason to fear that an independent, weak Japan could be a ready target for Communist encroachment. The structure of Japanese society was not fundamentally resistant to totalitarianism; there was a large industrial proletariat, sympathetic towards the Communist ideology,[76] and a high percentage of the intellectuals had

73. Dunn, p. 65.
74. *Ibid.*, p. 67.
75. *Ibid.*, pp. 76–84.
76. Collectivity orientation has remained a dominant part of the social environment of Japan. The traditional values laid stress on unconditional loyalty and obligations to the group, rather than on

leftist leanings. Furthermore, the practical economic benefits for Japan of friendship with the Soviet Union and the Chinese People's Republic could prove irresistable.

In seeking to keep Japan on her side, the United States became less concerned about obtaining Soviet cooperation.[77] In fact, with the peace treaty becoming a stratagem for security against the USSR, the securing of Soviet approval was no longer possible. At the same time, the USSR could not delay indefinitely the conclusion of a separate treaty between her wartime allies and Japan.

On 14 September 1950 President Truman announced that the State Department had been authorized to initiate discussions with member nations of the FEC regarding a Japanese peace treaty.[78] In a seven point memorandum sent to them, John Foster Dulles proposed that the peace treaty be formulated by any or all nations who had waged war with Japan and now were willing to make peace with Japan by means of bilateral discussion.

---

individual rights, on conformist harmony and orthodoxy rather than on free choice. In fact, the individual accepted the goals and aims of the collectivity and any distinction between the individual and the group tended to dissolve. These values were essentially alien to a liberal democratic approach. Again, the Japanese people had long been used to the unlimited extension of the functions of the State, reaching down to their private daily lives and regulating them. At the same time, there was a sense of distance which separated the masses from the centres of political power, retarding the growth of political maturity. The concentration of power in the hands of a few had been the tradition. All these traditional values made them responsive to a totalitarian system. The postwar reforms of institutional democratization had not succeeded in supplanting this strong heritage and instilling the spirit of individualism and democracy.

77. Borton, et al., *Far East*, p. 422.

78. Japan, Ministry of Foreign Affairs, Public Information Bureau, *Collection of Official Foreign Statements on Japanese Peace Treaty*, vol. 2, 14 September 1950 to 25 May 1951 (Tokyo, 1951), p. 1.

The Kremlin replied with a salvo of questions:

(1) The signatories of the Declaration of the United Nations on 1 January 1942 had undertaken not to conclude a separate peace. Did the United States contemplate a treaty in which only some of the powers would participate?

(2) Why should the question of Formosa, the Pescadores, the Kuriles and Sakhalin be subject to a fresh decision when it had already been decided by the Cairo Declaration, the Potsdam Declaration and the Yalta Conference?

(3) Why should Japanese sovereignty be removed from the Ryukyu and Bonin Islands, when the Cairo and Potsdam Declarations had made no mention of trusteeship?

(4) Would the treaty contain a definite programme of withdrawal of American troops?

(5) The Basic Surrender Policy of the FEC of 19 June 1947 prohibited the maintenance of an army, navy or air force by Japan. What was meant by the joint responsibility of the United States and Japan for the security of the latter?

(6) Was it the intention to remove all restrictions on Japan's development of a peacetime economy and grant her equal rights in world trade?

(7) What was being done to ascertain the views of the Chinese People's Republic?[79]

Thus the Soviet Union, without actually laying down the principles she wished incorporated in the peace treaty, advocated greater political and economic independence and welfare of Japan, while safeguarding her own interests in the Kuriles. Her insistence on a comprehensive

79. *Ibid.,* pp. 3–5, 117–120; Dunn, pp. 110–12.

treaty and the participation of Communist China in the peace conference echoed the sentiments of the Japanese people.

The United States responded on 27 December 1950 that the intention of the declaration in 1942 had been to prevent the conclusion of a separate peace while the war was still in progress. It could not be used by one nation to block any kind of peace treaty which it did not like. The United States contended that the territorial provisions of the war time agreements were subject to confirmation by the peace treaty. As regards trusteeship for the Ryukyus and Bonins, although no specific mention had been made of it in the Cairo and Potsdam declarations, the latter had stipulated that Japan would be limited to her four main islands and other small islands to be determined by the Allied Powers. The United States maintained that while the military occupation of Japan would be ended with the signing of the peace treaty, the retention of American troops in Japan for security purposes, under an agreement with the Japanese government, would be within the provisions of Article 51 of the United Nations Charter. She declared that she had no intention of putting any restrictions on the development of Japan's peacetime economy. The views of the Chinese People's Republic did not concern her, as she had not recognized its regime.[80]

A proposal by the USSR that the Council of Foreign Ministers of the Big Four be convened in June or July 1951 to lay the groundwork for a peace conference was killed by the United States on the ground that the Potsdam Agreement had not entrusted the Council of

80. Japan, National Diet Library, *Nisso kokko chosei mondai kiso shiryo shu* (Tokyo, 1955), pp. 33–34.

Foreign Ministers with settling the Japanese peace treaty. Yet the Soviet Union accepted the invitation to attend the San Francisco Peace Conference, determined to continue her opposition there. To the State Department's declaration on 16 August 1951 that the purpose of the San Francisco Conference was to conclude and sign the final text of the peace treaty and not reopen the discussion of its terms, the Soviet press and radio responded that Andrei Gromyko would nonetheless present new proposals for a Japanese peace treaty.[81]

It should be noted at this point that the popular belief that Japan was forced by the United States to conclude the Security Treaty as a price for achieving independence is false. The initiative for placing Japanese security in American hands had been taken by the Japanese government in the wake of the Soviet-American split out of fear that the United Nations would be unable to guarantee Japan's security.[82] Japan had exploited renewed Russo-American rivalry to secure American aid and obtain more favourable peace terms. In his talks at the Pentagon in May 1950 Ikeda Hayato had hinted that Japan might accept a Soviet peace treaty, if its provisions were more

81. For the full correspondence exchanged between the USSR and the United States regarding the treaty from December 1950, *see ibid.*, pp. 31–54.

82. Evidence of Okazaki Katsuo, permanent secretary in the Ministry of Foreign Affairs in the Katayama Cabinet, before the Commission on the Constitution on 6 May, 1959, *Kempo Chosa Kai dai 3 iinkai dai 30 kai sokai gijiroku*, pp. 2–4; Yoshida Memoirs, n. 2, pp. 264–68; *Kempo Chosakai*, pp. 5–7; It appears that Yoshida also got another draft treaty prepared in which he visualized Korea and Japan as demilitarized zones with a wide area around this zone being manned by forces of the USA, UK, China and Soviet Union. Depending upon world conditions, Yoshida proposed to use either of the two drafts. Evidence of Nishimura Kumao, former chief of the Treaty Bureau, in *Kempo Chosa Kai*, pp. 11–13.

favourable.[83] Little publicity had been given to the overtures of the Japanese government because the Japanese
public did not wish to see Japan committed to either side
in the Cold War,[84] lest she lose her freedom of action and
become the possible target of nuclear attack.

At the San Francisco Conference, which opened on 4
September 1951, the Soviet delegate insisted on Communist China's rights to Manchuria, Formosa and various
other islands off the China coast and on the USSR's rights
to the Kuriles and Sakhalin, while arguing for the return
of the Ryukyus and Bonins to Japan. He held that Japan
should not be allowed either to maintain substantial
armed forces or to conclude a military alliance with any
other country, and contended that the defence alliance,
contemplated in the treaty, was directed against the Soviet
Union and the Chinese People's Republic. He proposed
the demilitarization of the straits of La Pérouse (Soya),
Nemuro, Tsugaru and Tsushima and their opening to the
merchant vessels of all nations; passage of warships, on
the other hand, was to be restricted to those belonging
to the powers adjacent to the Sea of Japan.[85] As in the
Far Eastern Commission and in the Allied Council, so
at the San Francisco Peace Conference, however, the
Western powers politely listened to the Soviet wishes,
then ignored them in their decisions.[86]

In the final version of the peace treaty, Japan renounced all rights, titles and claims to Formosa, the

83. K. Miyazawa, "Ampo joyaku teiketsu no ikisatsu", *Chuokoron*,
May 1957, pp. 69–71.

84. Cole, pp. 650–51; editorials in *Asahi*, 14 January 1951, 23
January 1951; *Sekai*, December 1950, April 1951, August 1951, September 1951; *Chuo Koron*, September 1951.

85. For the full text of the speech, see *Nisso kokko chosei mondai*,
pp. 54–70, 72–75.

86. Dunn, pp. 183–5.

Pescadores and the Kurile Islands as well as to the portion of Sakhalin and the islands adjacent to it which she had acquired by the Treaty of Portsmouth, but no mention was made to whom the territories would be transferred. The objection of Japan's representative, Yoshida Shigeru, that the Southern Kuriles (Kunashiri and Etorofu) could not be said to have been seized by Japan through aggression and had been recognized by Imperial Russia as Japanese territory and that Habomai and Shikotan were part of Hokkaido had not been heeded.[87]

The Soviet Union boycotted the signing of the peace treaty on 8 September 1951.[88] While it would have been too late for her to prevent its signature and the signature of the Japanese-American Security Pact, the Soviet Union might have had a chance of thwarting ratification by the Diet had she offered to return to Japan the Kuriles and South Sakhalin and to conclude with her a neutrality treaty. But she was unwilling to part with these strategic gains even in an attempt to prevent Japan's alignment with the "Free World." With the ratification of the San Francisco Treaty, the Soviet Union suffered another setback in her competition with the United States for ascendency over Japan.

87. Yoshida's speech, *Nisso kokko chosei mondai*, pp. 75–78.

88. The treaty was finally signed on 8 September 1951 by 49 nations (including Japan), while the USSR, Czechoslovakia and Poland boycotted it. On the same day, Yoshida signed the Security Pact with USA. (Japan, Ministry of Foreign Affairs, *Treaty of Peace with Japan, Security Treaty between Japan and the United States of America* [*Annotated*] [Tokyo, 1951].)

MAP OF JAPAN
(REPRODUCED FROM JAPAN MINISTRY OF FOREIGN AFFAIRS
NORTHERN TERRITORIES 1970 P-4)

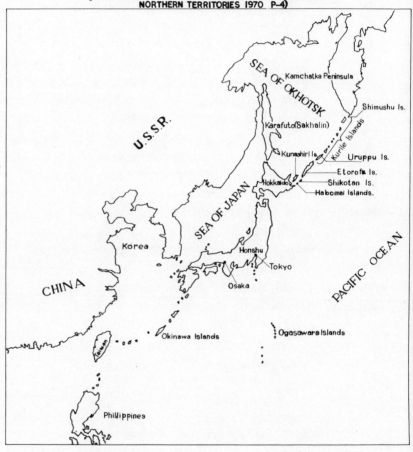

Scale :- 1cm=176km.

52

MAP OF THE NORTHERN ISLANDS
(UNDER DISPUTE BETWEEN JAPAN AND THE U.S.S.R.)

(REPRODUCED FROM JAPAN MINISTRY OF FOREIGN AFFAIRS
NORTHERN TERRITORIES 1970 P-5)

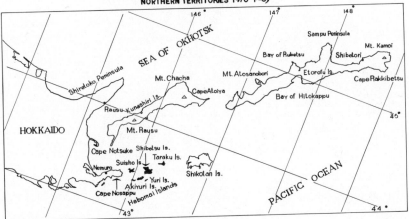

AREA :—

HOBOMAI GROUP OF ISLANDS 102 Sq. km.

SHIKOTAN   255 " "

KUNASHIRI   1,500 " "

ETOROFU   3,139 " "

　　　　TOTAL   4,996 " "

　　　　　　TWICE THE AREA OF OKINAWA

　　　　　　SCALE :- 1 cm = 15 km.

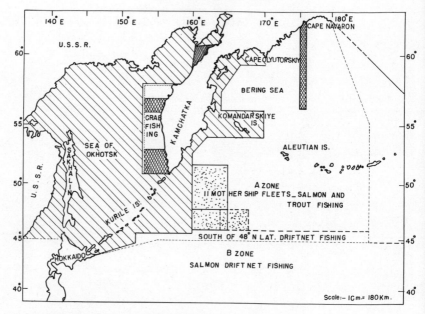

MAP SHOWING AREAS PROHIBITED FOR FISHING
AS AGREED TO
BY
JAPAN AND SOVIET UNION

LINE SHOWING THE A ZONE OF THE NORTH WEST PACIFIC
FISHERIES CONVENTION (Below this line B Zone)

AREAS PROHIBITED FOR SALMON TROUT FISHING

AREAS PROHIBITED FOR CRAB FISHING

MOTHER SHIP FISHING (Below this line drift net fishing)

NO FISHING AREA ONLY FOR 1966
(Every year it is agreed to declare some
part of this area off limits for fishing)

Foreign Minister Shigemitsu Mamoru
(Courtesy of Japanese Foreign Ministry)

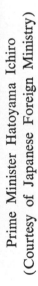

Prime Minister Hatoyama Ichiro
(Courtesy of Japanese Foreign Ministry)

Ambassador Matsumoto Shunichi
(Courtesy of Japanese Foreign Ministry)

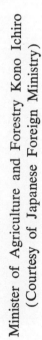

Minister of Agriculture and Forestry Kono Ichiro
(Courtesy of Japanese Foreign Ministry)

Signing of Trade and Payments Agreement, 2 March 1960.
(Courtesy of Japanese Foreign Ministry)

Signing of the Ninth Fisheries Agreement, 2 April 1965.
(Courtesy of Japanese Foreign Ministry)

Ambassador Oleg Troyanovsky at the Japan-Soviet Society, 23 March 1970
(Courtesy of *Nisso Kyokai*, Tokyo)

Fifteenth Convention of the Japan-Soviet Society.
(Courtesy of *Nisso Kyokai*, Tokyo)

Signing of the Basic Agreement for the Construction of the Port at Vrangel, 18 December 1970.

(Courtesy of Soviet Embassy, Tokyo)

2

Normalization of Relations

The San Francisco Peace Treaty and the Security Pact tied Japan to the democratic world. Article 26 of the peace treaty provided that Japan could not make another peace settlement granting greater benefits to any other state, without granting the same advantages to the parties of the San Francisco Treaty. Article 2 of the Security Pact stipulated that Japan would not grant any military bases to a third power without the prior consent of the United States.

Yet within Japan doubt continued about the government's alignment with the United States. Many people dreaded that Japan might be drawn into a conflict between the two blocs and perceived that it would be difficult to reestablish normal relations with their Communist neighbors. Although the treaty was ratified in the Diet by an overwhelming majority (307 voting for ratification, 47 against), a considerable number of delegates abstained (the House of Representatives had 486 members).[1] The continued presence of American troops after

1. *Survey 1951*, p. 418.

61

Japan had supposedly regained her independence hurt the national pride of many Japanese, irrespective of their ideological sympathies. Thus there was a climate of dissatisfaction and a budding anti-Americanism in Japan that the Soviet Union set out to exploit, depicting herself in her propaganda as singularly sympathetic to the peaceful aspirations of the Japanese people.

In awarding the Stalin Peace Prize to Oyama Ikuo of Japan in December 1951, the Soviet Union recognized the role played by "progressive" elements in Japan. Stalin lauded the struggle of these "progressive" elements against American imperialism in a New Year's message to Japan on 1 January 1952, a message prominently displayed at the Japanese Exhibition which was opened in Moscow that month[2] and widely discussed in the Japanese press.

The American State Department, Dean Acheson and John Foster Dulles in separate statements warned the Japanese people not to be taken in by peaceful protestations on the part of Stalin, reminding them of the attitude of the USSR toward the Emperor system, Soviet opposition during the Occupation to measures proposed by the United States for the removal of restrictions on Japanese development, Soviet intransigence on the repatriation question, continued Soviet occupation of the northern islands, and Soviet interference with Japanese fishing.[3] Premier Yoshida commented that Soviet goodwill could be demonstrated more effectively by actions than by words, such as by settling the repatriation problem and by refraining from inciting the Japanese Communists.[4]

2. *Asahi,* 3 January 1952; Japan, Cabinet Research Office, *Sovieto nenpo* 1955, pp. 659–61.

3. *Asahi,* 4 and 14 January 1952; *Mainichi,* 4 January 1952; *Tokyo,* 10 January 1952.

4. *Survey 1952,* pp. 364–65.

The Japanese press was of a divided mind regarding Stalin's New Year message and the peace offensive launched in Soviet newspapers. Some Japanese papers echoed the American view and denounced Soviet statements as sheer propaganda, others thought of the economic benefits that might accrue from relations with the Soviet Union and Communist China and advocated a policy of "eating the bait without actually being pulled up the line." There was also the feeling that the Soviet moves might reflect a change in policy, a tacit recognition of Japan's independence, and open the way for political and economic parleys between Japan and the USSR and the other Communist countries.[5]

With the restoration of Japanese independence, the Allied Council for Japan and the Far Eastern Commission were disbanded, even though the Soviet Union objected that since they had been established by an agreement of the Four Powers, consent of the Four Powers was required for their abolition.[6] This was no idle protest. In the absence of a peace treaty and thus of official diplomatic relations between the USSR and Japan, the dissolution of the Allied bodies deprived the Soviet mission of the right to remain in Japan.

An attempt by the Japanese government immediately following the ratification of the San Francisco Treaty on 24 April 1952 to deliver a note to the USSR through the Swedish government asking for the withdrawal of the Soviet mission failed when the Swedish government refused to accept it, as the USSR on an earlier occasion had not recognized Sweden's authority to represent Japanese

5. Editorials in *Yomiuri*, 4 January 1952; *Jiji*, 8 January 1952; and *Nihon Keizai*, 6 January 1952.

6. *Survey 1952*, p. 366; *Sovieto nenpo 1955*, p. 662; *Asahi* (evening), 29 April 1952.

interests. On 30 May 1952 the Japanese government handed a note to the Soviet mission in Japan asking it to leave. In its reply on 11 June 1952 the mission refused to do so, repeating the arguments the Soviet representatives had made at the final meetings of the ACJ and the FEC. Unable to expell the mission, Foreign Minister Okazaki Katsuo on 13 June 1952 deprived it of its special diplomatic rights. With the functions of the mission seriously curtailed by this action, the Soviet Union reduced its personnel to 16 persons, all of them civilians. The number eventually declined further as the Japanese government did not allow the entry into the country of any replacements for members who had to return to the USSR.[7]

The Soviet Union retained the mission to keep abreast of developments in Japan and to confer with various groups and individuals about economic relations and problems between Soviet and Japanese enterprises. In all its discussions, the mission stressed the theme that peace and stability in Northeast Asia could be achieved only through cooperation with the USSR.[8]

When the Japanese government had to allow visits by Japanese Red Cross officials and Diet members to the Soviet Union, the mission acted as an overseas agency. Later, when negotiations for the normalization of rela-

7. Sovieto nenpo 1955, pp. 662–63; Asahi, 16 and 31 May 1952; Yomiuri, 20 May 1952; Mainichi, 21 May 1952; (evening edition), 3 June 1952.

8. There were many organizations for promoting Soviet friendship, distribution of Soviet publications, translation of Soviet materials, exhibition of Soviet films. The most important were: Nisso Shinzen Kyokai (renamed Nisso Kyokai in June 1957), Nisso Gakujitsu Bunken Koryu Centre, and Nisso Tosho Kan.

These associations were clearly under Soviet and Communist control. For details of their activities, see Kyokutu Jijo Kenkyukai, Nisso koryu no haikei: Nisso kyokai to tainichi Rosen (Tokyo, 1958).

tions were begun, the mission was to function like an ordinary mission, transmitting the memoranda and verbal notes of its government to that of Japan, though the latter continued to send its replies directly to the Soviet Union. The hope of some Japanese that the question of the status of the mission might lead to a discussion of the normalization of relations with the USSR did not materialize.[9]

On 10 July 1952 Radio Moscow suggested that the Japan problem could be solved by the withdrawal of American troops and the granting of equal rights to other countries.[10] The notes exchanged between the Soviet Union and the Chinese People's Republic in the fall of 1952 stipulated the retention of Soviet troops in Port Arthur until a peace treaty between Japan, China and the USSR had been concluded.[11] The retention of Soviet troops in Manchuria as a counterweight to American troops in Japan dramatized the base issue, which was becoming a point of increasing dissension within Japan. Yet while popular discontent erupted in the bloody May Day riots in 1952, anti-American feeling could not be harnessed to the advantage of the USSR. Japan as a whole profited economically from the Korean War, and the presence of American troops, however galling psychologically, was good for the pocketbook.

9. "New Beginning in Soviet-Japanese Relations," *Asahi* editorial, 1 June 1952.

10. *Yomiuri* (evening), 10 July 1952.

11. *Sovieto nenpo 1955*, pp. 663–64; *Survey 1953*, p. 231. At the time of the Geneva Conference in April 1954 a member of the Chinese delegation told foreign correspondents that Russian troops in Port Arthur were there for the purpose of preventing aggression by Japan or by forces connected with Japan and that he thought that they should remain there till Japan became a truly democratic nation. (*Survey 954*, p. 241.)

The death of Stalin in March 1953 brought dramatic changes inside the USSR and ushered in a thaw in international relations. In a speech before the Presidium on 8 August 1953, Premier Georgy Malenkov declared that with the attainment of a truce in Korea, the time had come for the normalization of relations between the various countries in the Far East, especially between the Soviet Union and Japan.[12]

With the general improvement of East-West relations in 1954, the Soviet Union continued to give indications of her desire to normalize relations with Japan. She did not oppose Japanese entry into the Economic Commission for Asia and the Far East and invited Japan, as a member of ECAFE, to send delegates on a mission to inspect the agricultural and manufacturing industries of the USSR. The Japanese delegates reported upon their return that the Soviet Union seemed very keen on normalizing relations with Japan and developing trade.[13]

In a reply to a questionnaire from the Chubu Nippon Agency, Molotov stated in September 1954 that Japanese subservience to the United States was the main obstacle to the normalization of Soviet-Japanese relations. He expressed the view that Japan should have sufficient armed forces to defend herself alone, just like any other sovereign state.[14]

The joint Sino-Soviet communiqué issued on 12 October 1954 during Nikita Khrushchev's visit to Peking expressed the readiness of both countries to normalize relations with Japan. Revoking the arrangement made in September 1952 that Soviet forces remain in Port Arthur until the conclusion of a peace treaty between the

12. *Sovieto nenpo* 1955, p. 665.
13. *Ibid.*, pp. 667–68.
14. *Ibid.*, pp. 668–69.

USSR, China and Japan, the Russians agreed to return the area to China without compensation and to withdraw their troops by 31 May 1955.[15] The communiqué attributed the change in policy to the relaxation of tension in the world in general and to the truce in Korea and peace in Indo-China in particular. But it signified at the same time Soviet and Chinese realization that Japan could not be lured out of the American security system by threats. Dropping its insistence on the abrogation of the San Francisco Treaty, Moscow now stated, in line with its newly proclaimed policy of peaceful coexistence, that in seeking to normalize relations with Japan neither the Soviet Union nor China demanded that Japan discontinue the good relations she maintained with other countries.[16]

Within Japan herself there was increasing pressure for the normalization of relations with the Communist countries, as the end of the Korean War foreshadowed a drop in business, and a dollar shortage in the sterling bloc limited foreign purchases of Japanese goods.

Japanese trade with the USSR had been impeded at the time of the outbreak of the Korean War when the Western powers through the Coordinating Committee of the non-Communist bloc had banned the sale of strategic materials to the Soviet Union. It had been completely halted in early 1951, when the Kerr amendment to the Appropriations Act of that year had provided that no American economic or financial assistance could be provided to countries which exported to the USSR or other Communist countries articles banned by COCOM.[17]

15. *Ibid.*, pp. 669–70; *Survey of the China Mainland Press*, hereafter *SCMP*, 906, pp. 3–4.
16. *Sovieto nenpo 1955*, pp. 670–72.
17. *Documents 1951*, p. 43.

When the Soviet Union, in an effort to show how Japan could profit from trade with her, invited eight prominent Japanese businessmen to attend a world economic conference that was to be held in Moscow in April 1952, the Japanese government refused to issue them passports.[18]

Business circles were divided on the issue. The group under the leadership of *Keidanren* (Federation of Economic Organizations), headed by Ishikawa Ichiro, felt that no purpose would be served by attendance, while the group under the leadership of Murata Shozo favoured participation. The latter group appreciated the fact that the government could not commit itself politically, but it felt that private participation should be allowed, lest Japan be isolated from the rest of the world.[19] Although the government persisted in its refusal,[20] Kora Tomiko, a councillor of the Upper House who was in Paris for a UNESCO conference, went to Moscow to attend the world economic conference.[21]

Although the chief of the Japan-Soviet Trade Association, M. V. Nesterov, expressed Soviet interest in trade with Japan,[22] and although the prospect of a rouble market had a definite appeal as an alternative to American economic aid,[23] the Japanese government perferred cooperation with the United States to expanding trade with the Communist bloc. Only barter trade continued until the signing of an official trade agreement in 1957 in spite of the clamor of business circles and fishery interests for early normalization.

As long as Yoshida was at the helm of state, neither

18. *Asahi*, 19 January 1952.
19. *Jiji*, 2 February 1952.
20. *Jiji*, 9 February 1952.
21. *Asahi*, 7 April 1952.
22. *Sovieto nenpo 1955*, p. 662.
23. *New York Times Weekly*, 13 April 1952.

the activities of the Japanese interests groups nor the public statements made by the Soviet Union prodded the Japanese government into negotiations with the USSR. The conclusion of a Treaty of Friendship, Commerce and Navigation with the United States on 2 April 1953 restored the freedom of commercial activities by the nationals of either country in the territory of the other on a basis of most-favoured nation treatment[24] and the signing of the Mutual Defence Assistance Agreement a month later brought Japan 50 million dollars in American aid.[25]

With the fall of Yoshida and the formation of the Hatoyama government in December 1954, however, the situation changed. While Hatoyama Ichiro did not turn his back on the United States, he was determined to pursue a more independent policy.[26] Foreign Minister Shigemitsu announced on 11 December 1954 that Japan desired, without prejudice to her cooperation with the "Free World," "to normalize relations with the Soviet Union and China on terms mutually acceptable." But although Molotov replied in a Moscow broadcast that the USSR, as the Sino-Soviet communiqué of 12 October 1954 had stated, was ready for normalization if Japan truly desired it,[27] no diplomatic move by Japan followed.

It was the Soviet Union, therefore, which took the initiative and instructed her representative Andrei Ivanovich Dominitsky to deliver a note to the Japanese

24. The treaty went into effect on 30 October 1953. *United States Treaties and other International Agreements*, vol. 4, part 2, 1953, pp. 2063–2133.

25. *Survey 1953*, p. 273; *Documents 1953*, p. 464; *Documents 1954*, p. 356.

26. *Yoshitake Oka*, ed., *Gendai Nihon no seiji katei* (Tokyo, 1966), p. 92. The authors rightly feel that the change was only from a "policy of dependence [on the United States]" to an "amended policy of dependence."

27. *Mainichi*, 17 December 1954.

government. When the Foreign Office refused to receive it, Dominitsky approached Sugihara Kota, a member of the House of Councillors and a close friend of Hatoyama, through Kuhara Fusanosuke, president of the National Council of Associations for the Normalization of Relations with the Soviet Union and China (*Nichu Nisso Kokko Kaifuku Kaigi*). Hatoyama received Dominitsky at his residence on 7 January 1955, though Shigemitsu and the Foreign Office disapproved of such private overtures.

The Soviet note, which bore neither date nor signature, referred to the Sino-Soviet communiqué, the Molotov broadcast, as well as statements by Shigemitsu and Premier Hatoyama as indications that both sides were willing to enter into discussions and offered to appoint representatives to start negotiations either in Moscow or in Tokyo. While the note relieved Japan of the embarrassment of making the first formal move, she did not deem either capital acceptable as a location for the talks, since there was no Japanese mission in Moscow and no official Soviet mission in Tokyo. She proposed New York instead, but to this the Soviet Union did not agree. As a compromise London was chosen, and the talks were set for 1 June 1955, with Matsumoto Shunichi representing the Japanese side, Jacob Malik the USSR.[28]

When we analyze the position of the Japanese government on the eve of the talks, we find that there was a

28. Shunichi Matsumoto, *Moscow ni kakeru niji* (Tokyo, 1966), pp. 24–25. National Diet Library of Japan. *Nisso kokko chosei mondai kiso shiryo shu* (Tokyo, 1955), pp. 233–42, gives all the correspondence starting from Dominitsky's note till the final acceptance of London as the venue, including reports in *Pravda* and *Izvestiya*. The Japanese government verified the authenticity of the note by contacting the Soviet UN representative, A. N. Sobolev, through the Japanese UN representative, Sawada Renzo.

difference of approach in the stands taken by Hatoyama and Shigemitsu. While both agreed in principle that normalization should be effected, Hatoyama felt that the first step must be the termination of the state of war and the resumption of diplomatic relations; pending problems could be discussed thereafter on terms of equality. Shigemitsu, on the other hand, believed that if Japan passively accepted a declaration ending the state of war for the sake of resuming diplomatic relations, she would in effect acquiesce to Soviet occupation of Habomai and Shikotan. He argued, therefore, that Japan should first raise all pending issues and sound out Soviet opinion. Such a policy, he thought, would also prevent any misunderstanding on the part of the United States and the United Kingdom of Japanese motives.[29]

The Jiyuto Party warned that the Soviet overture was an attempt to drive a wedge between the United States and Japan and promised during the election campaign that it would stop negotiations with the USSR if returned to power. But public opinion was steadily moving in favour of ending the state of war, though it wished to proceed with caution.[30] It criticized both the stubborn noncooperation of the Jiyuto and Hatoyama's willingness to restore diplomatic relations without first solving the pending issues.[31]

Neither the United States nor the United Kingdom made any objections at this stage. In fact, the British Foreign Office commented that this was Japan's problem and that it welcomed all steps for relieving tension in Asia. James Reston of the *New York Times* wrote that the United States was not afraid that the Soviet Union

29. *Asahi*, 5 February 1955.
30. *Mainichi* (evening), 10 February 1955.
31. *Mainichi*, 22 May 1955; *Asahi*, 26 and 29 May 1955.

would be able to offer more concessions than she herself was offering. The world press in general interpreted the Soviet initiative as an attempt to capitalize on neutralist sentiment in Japan and Japan's response as a move to show her independence from the United States. The *Sydney Morning Herald* warned that the "Free World" must relax its trade restrictions if it wanted to keep Japan within its camp.[32]

The London talks began on 3 June 1955. There were fifteen sessions between that date and 13 September, when they were adjourned while Malik left for the United Nations and Matsumoto returned home for consultation. The negotiations were started on the basis of a Japanese memorandum which called for: (1) repatriation of all Japanese interned in the Soviet Union; (2) respect of Japan's rights and obligations under the San Francisco Treaty and the Security Pact; (3) return of the Habomai, Shikotan and Kuriles and South Sakhalin after the conclusion of a peace treaty; (4) freedom of fishing in the northern waters and the return of captured fishermen and boats; (5) an increase in economic relations, to be discussed in separate negotiations; (6) mutual respect for the principles set forth in the charter of the United Nations; and (7) Soviet support of Japan's entry into the United Nations.

On 16 August, during the eleventh session, Japan submitted a peace treaty draft, incorporating these provisions.[33] She did not consider her territorial demands as final, however. Matsumoto's instructions had stated that the unconditional return of Habomai and Shikotan would be satisfactory ground for the conclusion of a

32. *London Times*, 2 June 1955; *New York Times*, 3 June 1955; *Sydney Morning Herald*, 31 May 1955; *Times of India*, 2 June 1955.
33. Matsumoto, Appendix 8, pp. 186–90.

peace treaty. The return of the Southern Kuriles was to be demanded for historical reasons, but was not essential for an overall settlement; the Northern Kuriles and South Sakhalin were mentioned merely for bargaining purposes.[34]

The Soviets countered with a draft peace treaty of twelve articles:

1. The contracting parties mutually agree to respect each other's sovereignty and not to commit aggression against each other or to interfere in the internal affairs of each other.

2. The contracting parties mutually agree to respect the United Nations Charter and to settle all international disputes through peaceful means and not to endanger international peace and security.

   Japan agrees not to be a party to any alliance or military alliance directed against any of the countries which had participated in the war against her.

3. The Soviet Union agrees to renounce all claims for reparation from Japan in respect to the loss she and her people might have suffered in the period from 9 August 1945 till the end of the war through the activities of Japan and the Japanese people.

4. Japan also renounces all claims from the Soviet Union for any damages which she might have incurred during the period of the actual war and the state of war which existed in the Far East.

5. Japan recognizes the complete sovereignty of the Soviet Union in South Sakhalin, including the adjacent islands and the Kuriles, and re-

---

34. *Ibid.*, pp. 29–32; Donald Hellman, "Japanese Foreign Policy and Domestic Politics. The Peace Agreement with the Soviet Union," (MS, doctoral dissertation, University of California, Berkeley, 1964), pp. 136–37 and footnotes 41, 42.

nounces all her rights and claims in the above territories. The boundary between the Soviet Union and Japan will lie in the middle of Nemuro Strait, Notsuke Strait and Goyomai Strait.

6. (a) The contracting parties agree not to restrict the free navigation in Soya Strait, Nemuro Strait, Notsuke Strait and Goyomai Strait. Japan also agrees not to restrict free navigation in Tsugaru Strait and Tsushima Strait. The above straits will be open for the free commercial navigation of all countries.

(b) The above-mentioned straits will be open to warships only belonging to countries bordering on the Japan Sea.

7. The Soviet Union will support Japan's entry into the United Nations.

8. The contracting parties mutually agree to enter into negotiations for improving their economic relations and to conclude a Commercial and Navigation Treaty. Till such a Treaty is signed for eighteen months after this Treaty, the contracting parties agree to accord each other most favoured nation treatment in respect to tariffs, use of each other's ports for entry of vessels, fuelling, buying provisions for ships, etc.

9. The contracting parties mutually agree to enter into negotiations for concluding a Treaty or Agreement in respect to the catching of fish and other marine products, with the object of conservation of the marine life sources.

10. The contracting parties mutually agree to enter into agreement in respect to postal services, parcel posts, telephone services and wireless services.

11. The contracting parties agree to enter into negotiations for the conclusion of a cultural agreement with the object of fostering cultural cooperation and promoting mutual understanding.

12. This Treaty will have to be ratified and will become valid when the ratification documents are exchanged.[35]

In the process of negotiation it was revealed that the provision allowing only warships from countries bordering unto the Japan Sea to pass through the various straits had been inserted for bargaining purposes only. Thus the major points of disagreement in the Japanese and Soviet drafts concerned the territorial problem, the repatriation issue and the question of military alliance.

The Soviets claimed that the territorial issue had been settled by the Potsdam Declaration, the Yalta Agreement and SCAP Instructions No. 667. Matsumoto countered that Habomai and Shikotan had been enumerated separately from the Kurile Islands in SCAPIN 677 and that the latter had been only an order for military surrender and could not determine the territorial sovereignty of Japan. While Japan had relinquished the Kuriles and South Sakhalin in the San Francisco Treaty, the Soviet Union was not a party to that treaty; nor did the treaty transfer the territories to Soviet possession. He argued that these territories, therefore, were merely under Soviet occupation and that their ultimate disposition had not been decided.

On the question of participation in a military alliance, Matsumoto argued that the Japanese-American Security Pact was based strictly on the principle of individual and collective self-defence, recognized by the UN Charter, and was not directed against any country, as contrasted with the treaty of 1950 between the Soviet Union and China, which was clearly aimed at Japan. A provision in the peace treaty that Japan could not participate in any military alliance with any other nation would be an in-

35. Matsumoto, Appendix 6, pp. 183–86.

fringement on her sovereign rights and was, therefore, unacceptable.[36]

The Soviet Union withdrew the military pact clause
and promised to repatriate Japanese in the USSR, including sixteen war criminals. On 9 August 1955 Malik
expressed Soviet willingness to return the "small Kuriles,"
Habomai and Shikotan.[37] But when Matsumoto reported
this to the Japanese government, it stiffened its original
position, instructing him that a peace treaty could be
concluded only on the basis of the return of Habomai,
Shikotan and the Southern Kuriles and of an agreement
that the future of the remaining territories would be
decided by an international conference.[38] The Soviet
Union in turn became more rigid, inserting as a condition
for the return of Habomai and Shikotan the demand that
Japan undertake not to have any military bases on these
islands.[39]

The flexibility initially displayed by the Soviet Union
in the negotiations had conformed with the "spirit of

36. *Ibid.,* pp. 32–38; SCAPIN 677 stated in paragraph 3: "For the
purpose of this directive Japan is defined to include the four main
islands of Japan (Hokkaido, Honshu, Kyushu, Shikoku) . . . and
excluding . . . the Kurile Islands, the Habomai Island Group and
the Shikotan Island." (*Documents Concerning the Allied Occupation
and Control of Japan,* vol. 2, p. 24.)

37. Matsumoto, pp. 41–44.

38. Shigemitsu continued his go-slow policy and instructed Matsumoto to have talks only once a week instead of the initial proposal
of twice a week. Hatoyama was not kept informed of the details of
the negotiations. Shigemitsu made public the Soviet draft treaty,
against all diplomatic convention, and stated that its provisions were
the same as the proposals made by Gromyko in the San Francisco
Conference. The climate in Tokyo was explained to Matsumoto by
Kono on his way to Washington; Kono instructed Matsumoto not
to push the negotiations till his return from the United States. (Matsumoto, pp. 45–46.)

39. *Ibid.,* p. 49.

Geneva." Japan had not responded in kind, partly because of the views of the United States on the territorial
issue,[40] and partly because pressures within the Conserva-
tive Party required an expansion of Japan's territorial
claims for domestic political reasons. Needless to say,
Japan's demand for the return of the Southern Kuriles
did not sit well with the Russians. As Khrushchev told a
group of visiting Japanese Diet members, headed by
Kitamura Tokutaro, on 21 September, Japan did not
have any legal claims even to Habomai and Shikotan
and that the Soviet Union's offer to return them had been
due purely to her desire to promote good-neighbourly relations with Japan.[41] In December 1955 the USSR vetoed
Japanese admission to the United Nations, making it
plain that the normalization of relations between Japan
and the Soviet Union must precede Japan's entry into the
world body.[42]

The London talks were resumed on 9 January 1956

40. See the chapter on "The Northern Territories."
41. *Sovieto nenpo,* 1958, pp. 368–69; *CDSP,* vol. 7, no. 37, pp. 3–6.
42. Japan submitted her application for membership to the UN
on 16 June 1952. At the 601st Meeting of the Security Council, held
on 17 September 1952, the Soviet representative opposed Japan's
entry into the UN, stating that the USSR could support Japan's case
only when all foreign troops had been withdrawn and a multilateral
treaty signed. In 1955, the Soviet Union proffered to support Japanese membership in exchange for the admission of Outer Mongolia.
When the United States refused to link "a great nation like Japan
with a geographical abstraction like Outer Mongolia in a sordid
package deal," Japan's entry into the UN was again postponed.
(*SCOR,* yr. 7, mtg. 601, pp. 1–20; mtg. 602, pp. 1–15; *GAOR,*
Session 7, Plen. mtg. 410, pp. 474–79; Session 8, Annexes, Agenda
item 22, pp. 2–21; Session 8, Plen. mtg. 453, p. 252; Session 9, Plen.
mtg. 501, pp. 330–31; Session 10, Plen. mtg. 552, pp. 409–20; *SCOR,*
yr. 10, mtg. 701, pp. 1–21; mtg. 702, pp. 1–15; mtg. 703, pp. 1–13;
mtg. 704, pp. 1–22; mtg. 705, pp. 1–14; mtg. 706, pp. 1–22; mtg.
708, pp. 1–18.)

and continued until 20 March, with an interruption between 11 February and 8 March, when Malik visited Moscow to attend the Communist Party congress and consult with his government. During the eight sessions of the second London talks, Japan again failed to obtain Soviet agreement to deal with the repatriation problem apart from the treaty and to secure the return of the Southern Kuriles.

Matsumoto was on the verge of returning home for consultation, when Japan was shaken on 21 March by the publication of restrictions placed by the Soviet government on salmon and trout fishing in the Pacific. Justified as the measure may have been as a means of conserving the rapidly declining fish resources, it shifted attention from the territorial issue to the fishery problem.

At Matsumoto's suggestion special fishery talks were begun in Moscow on 29 April.[43] These will be discussed in a separate chapter, but it should be noted at this point that the USSR signed the Fishery Convention on 14 May 1956 on the express condition that the negotiations for the normalization of relations be resumed not later than 31 July 1956.

The normalization talks were duly reopened on 31 July, but moved for reasons of convenience to Moscow. Assisted by Matsumoto, Foreign Minister Shigemitsu now conferred directly with Foreign Minister Dmitry Shepilov. Yet the first Moscow talks, which lasted until 13 August 1956, brought no solution nearer.

The hard line which the Japanese government had expected and wanted Shigemitsu to follow,[44] merely stiffened the Soviet attitude. Neither Shepilov nor Khrushchev nor Nikolai Bulganin, chairman of the Council of

43. Matsumoto, pp. 75–98.
44. *Ibid.*, p. 102.

Ministers, whom Shigemitsu approached, were willing to cede more than Habomai and Shikotan, and they rebuffed any efforts to delete the final disposition of the northern territories from a peace treaty. When Shigemitsu, whether he saw no other way out or thought to better his political stature at home by a diplomatic coup, informed Shepilov on 12 August, without prior approval from Tokyo, that he would consider concluding the treaty on the lines indicated by the USSR and would give a detailed exposition of his views within three days,[45] the Japanese government angrily cabled him that a compromise at this stage would displease public opinion and the Jiyuminshuto (Liberal Democratic Party), and instructed him to ask for a recess in the talks to attend the Suez conference in London.[46]

When Shigemitsu met Shepilov in London on 18 August and told him that he was considering the Soviet proposal, Shepilov reiterated that the USSR would not go beyond the cession of Habomai and Shikotan. Shigemitsu was on the verge of agreeing when Secretary of State Dulles, who was also in London, intervened. He shocked Shigemitsu by warning him that if Japan accepted the Soviet proposal, she would in effect be granting to the USSR more concessions than contemplated by the San Francisco Treaty, and that the United States, in accordance with Article 26 of the treaty, would be constrained in such a case to annex Okinawa. Dulles asserted that the territories specified in the Yalta agreement could

45. *Ibid.,* pp. 105–10; Nanpo Doho Engo Kai ed., *Hoppo ryodo mondo kiso shiryo* (Tokyo, 1958), pp. 126–29; Hellman, p. 143; Ichiro Kono, *Imadakara hanaso* (Tokyo, 1958), pp. 55–56; *Japan Times,* 12 August 1956.

46. Matsumoto, pp. 111–5; *Mainichi,* 1, 11 and 13 August 1956; *Asahi,* 5 August 1956, *Sankei* 8 and 14 August 1956.

not be ceded to the Soviet Union without a separate peace treaty and that the USSR, therefore, had no basis for demanding that Japan recognize Soviet sovereignty in those territories.[47] Dulles' threat strengthened the position of those who opposed coming to terms with the Russians, lest a détente with the USSR impair Japanese-American relations.[48] Yet the Japanese government did not turn its back on the USSR. The Moscow talks had merely been recessed, and a number of officials had remained in Moscow for liaison.

On 19 August 1956 Hatoyama announced that if the ruling party and the government considered it proper, he was prepared to visit Moscow, if his health permitted.[49]

Agriculture Minister Kono Ichiro and the early advocates of the normalization of relations with the USSR strongly supported such a trip by Hatoyama, while the old Jiyuto group roundly condemned it.[50] Hatoyama's supporters believed that once he had solved the thorny issue of restoring relations with the USSR, Hatoyama could retire from politics gracefully; his opponents feared

47. At a news conference on 28 August 1956 Dulles denied that he had made any specific statement to Shigemitsu that the United States might demand sovereignty over Okinawa, if Japan recognized the Soviet claim to the Kuriles. (*DSB,* 10 September 1956, p. 406.) The Japanese Ambassador in Washington had been told the same as Shigemitsu. Dulles asserted on 24 August 1956 that he had only meant to strengthen Japan's bargaining position. (Matsumoto, pp. 116–17). The American *aide memoire* of 7 September 1956 stated that Japan did not have the right to transfer sovereignty over the territories renounced by her in the San Francisco Peace Treaty. (*DSB* 17 September 1956, p. 484.)

48. Yoshida declared that the Dulles statement to Shigemitsu showed American displeasure of Hatoyama's pro-Soviet views. (*Sankei,* 23 August 1956, morning and evening editions.)

49. Matsumoto, p. 120.

50. *Asahi,* 4 September 1956; *Mainichi,* 5 September 1956; *Nihon Keizai,* 6 September 1956.

that he would take advantage of the popularity that such success would bring to become president of the party. Only when Hatoyama pledged to retire once normalization of relations had been attained, did his mission to Moscow receive the necessary full support.[51]

To avoid a new deadlock on the territorial problem, the Japanese government proposed to discuss the following five questions: (1) Ending the state of war; (2) establishment of diplomatic relations; (3) early repatriation of Japanese interned in the Soviet Union; (4) implementation of the fishery agreement; and (5) Soviet support of Japanese entry into the United Nations. The Soviet representative in Tokyo, Sergei Chivinsky, told Kono and Matsumoto informally that the Soviet Union would not be averse to resuming negotiations on this basis. Accordingly, Hatoyama sent Bulganin a note on 11 September 1956 stating that the Japanese government was prepared to normalize relations between the two countries, provided that agreement was reached on the above-mentioned five issues, with the territorial question being left for future consideration. It was proposed that the points of agreement negotiated in London should be adopted as far as possible.

Bulganin replied on 13 September that the Soviet Union accepted the Japanese proposition.[52] Since his letter made no specific reference to the condition that the territorial question be left for consideration at a later date, however, Matsumoto was dispatched to Moscow to obtain clarification. The Gromyko-Matsumoto correspondence, which was made public later, reveals that the USSR was indeed willing to leave the territorial question

51. *Asahi* 7, 8, 9 September 1956; Tadao Yanaihara (ed.), *Sengo Nihon sho shi* (Tokyo, 1961), vol. 2, p. 366.
52. Matsumoto, pp. 121–24; pp. 201–3.

for later consideration as part of a formal peace treaty and begin with the restoration of diplomatic relations.[53]

No further objections could be raised to the Hatoyama mission, and the delegation left for Moscow, where it arrived on October 12. Hatoyama's instructions included a policy directive prepared by the Japanese government, which reiterated the desirability of concluding a peace treaty containing a settlement of the territorial issue, namely the immediate return of Habomai and Shikotan and the restoration of the Southern Kuriles after Okinawa had been returned to Japan by the United States. Japan was to renounce her rights in the Northern Kuriles and South Sakhalin. If a peace treaty with such provisions could not be obtained, a Basic Treaty might be concluded, incorporating all the issues on which agreement had been reached in London. In such an event Soviet assent should be procured for the consideration of the territorial issue as part of a peace treaty at a later date. If the USSR objected to the conclusion of a Basic Treaty, the same provisions could be included in "open letters" to be exchanged by the two governments and to be validated through ratification.[54]

During the negotiations in Moscow, Kono tried to prevail on the Fisheries Minister, A. A. Ishkov, as well as on Khrushchev himself, that Habomai and Shikotan should be returned immediately, Kunashiri and Etorofu upon the return of Okinawa by the United States. Khrushchev reminded him that it had been agreed in the Gromyko-Matsumoto correspondence not to deal with the territorial question for the present. If provision regarding Habomai and Shikotan were to be inserted, Japan would have to agree to conclude a peace treaty and not a joint declara-

53. Text in Matsumoto, pp. 203–205.
54. *Ibid.*, pp. 139–42.

tion. Pressed for a commitment about Habomai and Shikotan, Khrushchev drafted a pledge that they would be returned after a peace treaty had been signed and after Okinawa had been returned by the United States, though he expressed willingness to make a gentlemen's agreement that they would be returned upon the conclusion of a peace treaty, without reference to Okinawa. Hatoyama was no more successful in obtaining pledges for the return of additional territory from Bulganin.

When Kono put forward a draft agreement that Japan and the Soviet Union would start negotiations for a peace treaty *including territorial issues* after diplomatic relations had been restored and that the Soviet Union, acceding to Japanese demands and taking into consideration the interests of Japan, agreed to return Habomai and Shikotan upon the conclusion of a peace treaty, Khrushchev demanded the omission of the words "including territorial issues." To Kono's reply that they were very important, as the ruling party placed great emphasis on the territorial question, Khrushchev retorted that in such a case it should be stated that the return of Habomai and Shikotan after the peace treaty would constitute a settlement of the territorial issue between the two countries. Since Kono would not agree to this, Khrushchev stated that the earlier draft and the above-mentioned gentlemen's agreement constituted the maximum Soviet concession.

After further consideration, Kono proposed the following solution:

(1) clear mention in the Joint Declaration that Habomai and Shikotan would be returned at the conclusion of a peace treaty;

(2) publication of the Gromyko-Matsumoto correspondence of 29 September 1956; and

(3) deletion of the words "including territorial issues" from the Joint Declaration.

The Soviet Union accepted this compromise, including return of Habomai and Shikotan in the Joint Declaration without any reference about the disposition of further territory one way or another.[55] The solution aroused opposition in Tokyo among the old Jiyuto group in the ruling Jiyuminshuto. Since most members of the mainstream (old Minshuto) believed such a compromise to be inevitable and its conclusion a means of obtaining Hatoyama's early retirement,[56] a concensus was reached once again on the basis of intra-party policies rather than national interest.

Hatoyama had obtained from Bulganin the pledge that the USSR would support Japan's entry into the United Nations. Matsumoto succeeded in deleting from the final declaration the provision in the Soviet draft that "after discussion of the various international problems, the two countries were of the same views." The various points on which Malik and Matsumoto had reached agreement in London in March were included in the final draft.[57]

The Joint Declaration was signed on 19 October 1956.

55. *Ibid.*, pp. 143–49. It should be pointed out in this connection that Hatoyama and Kono did not make it clear during the interpellations in the special committee constituted for discussing the declaration, that the Okinawa question was linked up with the return of the Kuriles. When pressed whether it was not brought up at all, they took shelter by saying that it was not in the public interest to disclose the details of the negotiations. (Japan, House of Representatives, 25th Session *Proceedings of Meeting of Special Committee on Joint Declaration with the Soviet Union,* 20 November 1956.) However, Khrushchev disclosed in an interview with the chief editor of *Asahi* that the return of Okinawa had been linked with the return of the northern territories. (*Pravda,* 30 June 1957, in *CDSP* vol. 9, no. 26, pp. 3–7.)

56. Matsumoto, pp. 151–52.

57. *Ibid.*, pp. 149–51.

It provided, *inter alia,* for an end of the state of war, restoration of diplomatic relations, regulation of mutual relations according to the UN Charter, Soviet support of Japan's entry in the UN, repatriation of Japanese detainees, mutual relinquishment of the right for reparations, early negotiations for concluding a Treaty of Commerce and Navigation, affirmation of the validity of the Fisheries Agreement signed on 14 May 1956, and early negotiation of a peace treaty followed by the return of Habomai and Shikotan.[58]

The wording of the provision regarding the return of Habomai and Shikotan deserves special note: "The Union of Soviet Socialist Republics, in response to the desire of Japan and in consideration of her interests, agrees to transfer the Habomai Islands and the islands of Shikotan to Japan, provided, however, that the actual transfer of these islands shall be effected after the peace treaty between Japan and the Union of Soviet Socialist Republics is concluded." While it had been understood by the Japanese throughout the discussions that the islands would be returned at the time of or along with the conclusion of the peace treaty, the use of the word "after" in the Joint Declaration left the date of return unclear.

The final settlement made by Hatoyama was in no way more favourable than the terms attained earlier by Matsumoto or Shigemitsu. After sixteen months of negotiation Japan had failed to achieve the actual return of Habomai and Shikotan or agreement in principle that the disposition of the Southern Kuriles might be subject to discussion at a later date; the Soviets in turn had not obtained Japanese recognition of Soviet sovereignty over the northern territories.

58. For the full text of the Joint Declaration see Appendix C.

The repatriation problem also remained an irritant in the relations between the two countries for a number of years.[59] In vain Japan had tried to separate it from the issue of a peace treaty. Her contention that, since she had not invaded the Soviet Union, it was not proper for the latter to detain Japanese as war criminals and link the issue with the peace treaty as had been done in the case of Germany, had been rebuffed by Malik with the argument that because Japan had surrendered unconditionally, the repatriation problem would have to be settled along with the peace treaty.[60]

As mentioned already, the Soviet Union had begun repatriating Japanese in 1946, but though she had promised in an agreement with the United States to return 50,000 persons a month, she had not lived up to the schedule and had subjected the detainees to indoctrination before returning them. On 22 April 1950 the USSR had announced that she held only nine sick persons and 2,458 war criminals; she had returned the sick men and halted further repatriation.[61] But in November 1953 repatriation had been resumed through the good offices of the Japanese Red Cross.

The problem was that no one knew how many prisoners were involved. A list which Malik produced on 5 September 1955 during the London talks contained only 1,364 names, while the list prepared by Japan included

---

59. *Mainichi* polls of 14–16 October 1955 showed that 40.9 per cent gave first priority to the repatriation problem. (*Mainichi*, 24 October 1955.) When the negotiations were temporarily suspended, polls on 15–17 June 1956 showed that the repatriation problem was placed ahead of the territorial problem. (*Mainichi*, 12 July 1956.)

60. Matsumoto, pp. 32–33, 77–78.

61. *Sovieto nenpo 1958*, p. 376; *GAOR*, Session 5, Annexes, Agenda item 67, pp. 15–18; Session 5, Plen. mtg. 325, pp. 668–69.

11,177 persons.[62] It is difficult to accuse the Soviet Union of deleting names from her list in order to hold on to the prisoners or Japan of padding lists to inflame anti-Soviet sentiments. The confused conditions prevailing after the war made the task of compiling an accurate list impossible, as did the fact that many Japanese prisoners, in order to avoid detention and forced labor, had passed themselves off as North Koreans and had married Korean or Russian women and decided not to return.[63]

Soviet reluctance to separate the repatriation question from the peace treaty issue may have been due to the desire to pressure the Japanese government into an early normalization of relations. Once the Joint Declaration had been signed, the USSR agreed to return all detained Japanese and to investigate the whereabouts of those considered missing. She lived up to the promise and although the search for missing Japanese may never be completed, it appears that all detainees desirous of returning home were repatriated.[64]

In negotiating with the Russians, the policy of the Japanese government had not always reflected public opinion. The public, like the government, had favoured the restoration of diplomatic relations prior to a settlement of the territorial problems.[65] There was, however,

---

62. *Ibid., Sovieto nenpo 1958*, p. 376. Even while the negotiations were going on, the Soviet Union was releasing people in small groups in accordance with the Red Cross Agreement. (*Pravda*, 26 August 1956, in *CDSP*, vol. 8, no. 34, p. 19.)

63. *Asahi*, 20 October 1956.

64. The Presidium of the Supreme Soviet ordered the release and repatriation of all sentenced Japanese. (*Pravda*, 14 December 1956, in *CDSP* vol. 8, no. 50, p. 51.) For details of repatriation, see *Sovieto nenpo 1959*, pp. 378–79 and "Nisso Kankei no keiei to so no genjo," in Japan, Cabinet Research Office, *Chosa geppo*, June 1966, pp. 11–12.

65. *Manichi*, 24 October 1955; *Asahi*, 7 December 1955; *Yomiuri*, 20 April, 22 September 1956.

a strong popular demand for the return of all the northern territories and opposition to an agreement for the return of Habomai and Shikotan only.[66] Although the repatriation problem was close to the heart of the people and there was unanimous feeling that steps should be taken for early repatriation of Japanese in the Soviet Union, the Japanese government had not been willing to agree to the restoration of diplomatic relations on the basis of the settlement of that issue alone.[67]

During the negotiations Japan had displayed a tendency of overestimating her importance, blind to the fact that her bargaining position was weak. Every important issue under negotiation had affected her interests more than those of the Soviet Union. Yet the tenor of her statements in discussing the resumption of diplomatic relations had been such that the Soviet delegate had felt compelled repeatedly to remind her that she had lost the war and had surrendered unconditionally.[68]

As the negotiations had dragged out and the Soviet Union had resorted to the repatriation and fishery questions as levers for reaching a settlement, much criticism had been heaped upon her. The press practically ignored the hardening of the Japanese government's policy on the territorial issue and the expansion of its territorial claims and gave full blame to the Soviet Union for refusing to part with Japanese territory. The settlement, therefore, came as a disappointment to the public and did not increase the popularity of the Soviet Union. In fact, anti-Communists voiced fear that the restoration of diplomatic

66. *Yomiuri*, 9 August, 1 December, 20 April 1956; *Mainichi*, 24 October, 12 July 1956; *Asahi*, 2 September 1956.

67. *Nihon Keizai*, 3 April 1956; *Asahi*, 31 March 1956.

68. Khruschchev interview with the Japanese Diet delegation on 21 September 1955 in *CDSP*, vol. 7, no. 37, p. 4; remarks by Malik at the London conference in Matsumoto, pp. 77–78.

relations would open Japan to espionage and subversion and demanded a strengthening in internal security measures.[69]

The Japanese House of Representatives ratified the Joint Declaration on 27 November 1956 by a vote of 365 to 0, with 82 members absenting themselves. The House of Councillors ratified the declaration on 5 December by a vote of 227 to 3. The ratification instruments were exchanged in Tokyo a week later, on 12 December. The same day, the Security Council adopted a resolution recommending Japan's entry into the United Nations.[70] Yet Hatoyama's resignation on 14 December 1956 opened the way to power for a faction more favourably disposed toward the United States and the prospects of better political relations with the Soviet Union appeared dim.

Let us look at the economic consequences of the re-establishment of formal relations with the USSR on Soviet-Japanese trade and on the perennial northern fisheries questions and see whether they provided the Soviet Union with a chance to better her image and counteract the influence of the United States.

69. *Sankei,* 22 March 1955, feature article; *Asahi,* 21 October and 20 November 1956; *Nihon Keizai,* 11 November 1956.

70. *Asahi nenkan* 1957, pp. 285–86; *SCOR,* yr. 11, supplement for October-December 1956, p. 145; *GAOR,* Session 11, supplement no. 17, p. 60.

3

Japanese-Soviet Trade

Japanese trade with the Soviet Union had always been small in comparison with her trade with the United States. Prior to the Manchurian Incident Japanese exports to the United States had accounted for about 40 per cent of Japan's total exports, imports from the United States for about 30 per cent of her total imports. After 1932, however, America's share of Japanese exports had declined sharply to about 20 per cent of her total exports, though imports had remained at about the same level. The United States had supplied Japan raw cotton, petroleum, iron, and other raw materials essential for Japanese industry and, as Japan had begun to prepare for war, with scrap iron, copper, steel sheets, crude and heavy oils, and motor cars.[1]

In comparison, Japanese trade with the Soviet Union had amounted at its peak to only 1.9 per cent of Japan's total export trade and 2.5 per cent of her total imports, with Asiatic Russia taking about 95 percent of the exports

1. Mitsubishi Economic Research Bureau, *Japanese Trade and Industry Present and Future* (London, 1936), pp. 591–94.

to the USSR. Japanese exports to the Soviet Union had included green tea, fishing nets and other fishing equipment, steel products, metal manufactures, machinery and tools; Japanese imports had consisted mainly of salted fish and shell fish, coal, manganese, mineral oil, and timber. Except for the period from 1935 to 1937, when Japan had exported a large number of goods in partial payment for the Chinese Eastern Railway, she had had an unfavourable balance of trade with the USSR in prewar days.[2]

The Pacific War destroyed the "yen bloc" which Japan had built up, and she was forced to look for new markets and suppliers. But she was not a free agent, her foreign trade being under the direct control of SCAP; from April 1947 till the end of 1949 it was conducted through official trading corporations.

Japanese trade with the Soviet Union between 1946 and 1949 was as follows:[3]

(in thousand dollars)

Year	Export	Percentage of total exports	Imports	Percentage of total imports
1946	24	0.02	0	
1947	140	0.08	2,004	0.6
1948	4,385	1.70	2,670	0.5
1949	7,360	1.40	1,933	0.2

2. *Ibid.*, pp. 585–88, Nisso To-O Boeki Kai, ed. *Nisso boeki yoran nenkan 1959* (Tokyo, 1958), pp. 223–25; *Sovieto nenpo 1955*, pp. 676–79. See also George Alexander Lensen, "The Russian Impact on Japan," in Wayne S. Vucinich (ed.), *Russia and Asia* (Stanford, 1972), 344–48, and G. A. Lensen, *The Damned Inheritance: The Soviet Union and the Manchurian Crises, 1924–1935* (Tallahassee, 1973), Appendix A.

3. Japan, Office of Prime Minister, Bureau of Statistics, *Japan Statistical Yearbook* (1949).

Most of the export trade was accounted for by the repair of boats or the supplying of boats, engines and manila rope. Imports consisted of coal, coke and santonin.[4]

In 1950 the Soviet Union wanted to place orders for Japanese textile machinery, tankers, freighters, small and big cranes, and electric motors, but SCAP refused to entertain further Soviet orders until the USSR had paid the four million dollars she owed. The Soviet Union wanted to pay in kind, but of the products she offered, Japan only needed the coal from Sakhalin. A one million dollar agreement was signed for the supply of 100,000 tons of coal, but only 74,000 tons were delivered.[5]

In 1951 SCAP allowed direct Japanese-Soviet negotiations for trade on a barter basis. COCOM restrictions that were introduced with the outbreak of the Korean War, however, stifled trade with the USSR.[6]

4. *Nisso boeki yoran*, p. 226.
5. *Sovieto nenpo* 1955, p. 681.
6. Unilateral action by the United States to retard the military build-up of the Soviet Bloc by denying her selected strategic goods was considered insufficient and in 1949 this was transferred to a multilateral forum, and an informal Consultative Group (CG) was formed in Paris by the UK, France, Italy, the Netherlands, Belgium, Luxembourg and the United States. The membership was subsequently expanded to include Norway, Denmark, Canada and the Federal Republic of Germany and eventually Portugal, Greece, Turkey and Japan. Two subordinate working committees performed the task of co-ordinating free trade controls, overseeing enforcement and recommending improvement measures. One was the Co-ordinating Committee (COCOM), established in January 1950 and concerned with trade controls applying to the European Soviet Bloc; the other was the China Committee (CHINCOM) established in September 1952 with controls over shipment to Communist China, North Korea and North Vietnam, controls which were more extensive and stringent than those in effect against the European Soviet Bloc. There were three lists, List I (embargo), List II (quantitative controls) and List III (surveillance). The activities of COCOM were kept

Although the Soviet government issued invitations to Japanese businessmen for the World Economic Conference held in Moscow in 1952, and though the Soviet mission in Tokyo sought to persuade Japanese businessmen and Diet members of the desirability of expanded economic relations with the Soviet Union, a glance at the following figures[7] reveals that total trade did not substantially increase until 1955.

(in thousand dollars)

Year	Export	Import	Balance
1950	723	738	−15
1951	0	28	−28
1952	150	459	−309
1953	7	2,101	−2,094
1954	39	2,249	−2,210
1955	2,067	3,073	−1,006
1956	760	2,869	−2,109
1957	9,295	12,326	−3,031

The above figures do not include ship repairs, which brought the barter trade into balance.[8]

Looking at Japan's trade with the USSR in the context of Japan's overall foreign trade revival, we find that the official index of the quantum of imports and exports (1934–36 = 100) was only 4.3 for imports, and 7.4 for exports in 1946.[9] While the slow growth of foreign trade

---

secret. Provisions for relaxation of the lists were authorized on the basis of prior consultation, before and after notification and special justification. (*The Strategic Trade Control System 1948–56; Mutual Defence Assistance Control Act, 1951; Ninth Report to Congress, 1957*, pp. 1–22.)

7. *Chosa geppo*, June 1966, p. 17.
8. *Nisso boeki yoran*, p. 230.
9. Hitotsubashi University, Institute of Economic Research, ed.,

in general might partly explain the slow increase in trade with the USSR, there were other factors which contributed to its stagnation.

The Soviet Union pursued a policy of autarky, limiting her imports as much as possible. Furthermore, she subordinated her trade relations to political considerations, and held out the prospects of increased trade as an enticement for the conclusion of a peace treaty. Besides, Japanese trade would have been most profitable, in terms of proximity with Siberia and the Russian Far East, but these regions were as yet underdeveloped.

On the Japanese side too, conditions were unfavourable until 1956 for the development of Japanese-Soviet trade. The American Occupation, American financial and economic aid and technological know-how made it natural for Japan to look to the United States as her major trade partner. Large American orders in Japan during and after the Korean War intensified the process[10] and made Japanese businessmen cautious not to endanger the profitable dealings with the United States.[11] At the same time, the delay in normalization of relations with the USSR prevented exploratory visits by Japanese business leaders to that country. Soviet trade representatives were not allowed to enter Japan until August 1954, and then stayed only for sixty days to avoid finger printing, which carries a bad connotation in their country.[12]

Annotated Economic Statistics of Japan for Post-war Years up to 1958 (in Japanese) (Tokyo, 1960), p. 84; G. C. Allen, *Japan's Economic Expansion* (London, 1965), p. 238.

10. Allen, *Japan as a Market and Source of Supply* (London, 1967), pp. 385–403. Allen, *Japan's Economic Expansion*, p. 229.

11. The United States government had decreed that vessels and persons that had touched Communists ports could not enter American ports. (*Oriental Economist*, June 1954, p. 269.)

12. *Oriental Economist*, September 1954, p. 458; September 1956, p. 455.

The restrictions imposed by COCOM hindered the development of trade with the USSR. Although the COCOM prohibitions were relaxed in 1954, the restrictions on the sale of ships, which could have played a large role in Japanese-Soviet trade, were continued.[13] Other commodities now could be exported, but the Soviet Union preferred British, West German and Belgian heavy machinery, which was better in quality and cheaper in price.[14] The felling of trees on Hokkaido by a typhoon in 1954[15] and the switch to domestic timber in the production of rayon pulp reduced the Japanese demand for Soviet timber.[16]

The Soviet practice of quoting the "international price" for her exports—the European market price in the case of raw cotton and petroleum, the American market price in the case of Sakhalin coal—nullified the competitive advantage the USSR might have had in view of her proximity and state-controlled economy.[17] Finally, the settling of barter trade accounts was cumbersome.[18] It was evident, therefore, that the development of viable economic relations between Japan and the USSR required the conclusion of a formal economic agreement.

The Joint Declaration of 19 October 1956 provided in Article 7 for the commencement of negotiations for a

13. *The Strategic Trade Control System*, pp. 23–28; *Oriental Economist*, September 1956, p. 455.

14. *Oriental Economist*, July 1954, p. 357; *Sovieto nenpo 1955*, p. 684.

15. *Nisso boeki yoran*, p. 230.

16. Allen, *Japan as a Market*, p. 40.

17. *Sovieto nenpo 1955*, p. 683.

18. For a discussion of various trade formulas, see *Oriental Economist*, June 1958, p. 297; Chugoku Kenkyujo, ed., *Nichu Nisso boeki no shin tenkai* (Tokyo, 1954), pp. 26–30; *Sovieto nenpo 1955*, p. 684; Raymond F. Mikesell and Jack N. Behrman, *Financing Free World Trade with the Sino-Soviet Bloc* (Princeton, 1958), pp. 48–49.

Commercial Treaty. A trade protocol signed at the time gave to the Soviet Union and Japan most-favoured-nation treatment in the import and export of goods and the entry of ships into each other's harbours, and made detailed provisions for the quantity of trade, exchange regulations, and payment procedures.

The prediction of Shepilov during the second Moscow negotiations that Soviet-Japanese trade might reach one billion roubles aroused interest in Japan. The projection appeared plausible as the sixth Five Year Plan, adopted in February 1956, envisioned the development of Siberia and the Russian Far East, in which Japan could play a special role. The long-term development of the region held out to neighbouring Japan the prospect of huge supplies of raw materials, such as petroleum, coal, and timber, as well as a vast market for Japanese consumer goods and machinery.

Negotiations were begun in Tokyo on 12 September 1957. An attempt by the Japanese side to confine the Soviets, with their monolithic economy, to dealing with a special State Trading Agency that the Japanese wanted to establish for that purpose, was rebuffed by the Russians on the ground that it would block direct contacts between Soviet trade organizations and Japanese trading firms and would be in contravention of the most-favoured-nation status, embodied in the Joint Declaration.[19]

On 6 December 1957 a Treaty of Commerce was concluded for a period of five years, granting most-favoured-nation treatment in respect to customs duties, levies, procedures, and regulations.[20] The stipulation that no im-

19. *Oriental Economist,* October 1957, p. 535; *Sovieto nenpo 1959,* pp. 373–75; *Pravda,* 20 November 1957, in *CDSP,* vol. 9, no. 47, pp. 14–15.

20. For the text of the Treaty of Commerce, see *The Japanese Annual of International Law 1958,* pp. 173–83.

port and export restrictions should be imposed on trade with the Soviet Unon that were not also imposed on trade with other nations was modified by the clause that the contracting parties could take measures to protect their security; thus the COCOM embargo remained in effect.

A document appended to the commercial treaty made the Soviet Trade Mission part of the embassy, extending to it diplomatic status and the right to use code.[21] A Trade and Payments Agreement, signed at the same time, provided for payment in pounds sterling, with barter trade to be allowed in exceptional cases.

The Treaty of Commerce went into effect on 9 May 1958. The following month, on 3 June, an agreement was signed, establishing a sea route between the ports of Yokahama and Nakhodka and between Japan and the Black Sea.[22]

Following the conclusion of the Treaty of Commerce, Japan's trade with the USSR compared with her total foreign trade and her trade with the Communist Bloc as follows:[23]

(in million dollars)

Year	Total Foreign Trade	Trade with Communist Bloc	Proportion of trade with Communist Bloc to total trade	Trade with Soviet Union	Proportion of Soviet trade to total trade
	A	B	B/A (%)	C	C/A (%)
1958	5,907	161	2.7	40	0.07
1959	7,055	107	1.5	62	0.09

21. The Trade Mission had a staff of 22 besides the trade representative and his two assistants. The Embassy staff was reduced by 5 members bringing it to 50 not counting the Trade Mission personnel. (*Sovieto nenpo 1959*, pp. 375–76).

22. *Sovieto nenpo 1959*, pp. 374–6.

23. *Chosa geppo*, June 1966, p. 19; Japan, Ministry of International Trade and Industry, *Tsusho hakusho*, 1969, 1970, 1971.

1960	8,546	198	2.3	147	1.7
1961	10,046	320	3.1	210	2.1
1962	10,553	440	4.1	296	2.3
1963	12,191	534	4.3	320	2.6
1964	14,610	830	5.7	408	2.8
1965	16,620	1.004	6.0	408	2.5
1966	19,299	1,287	6.7	514	2.6
1967	22,104	1,394	6.3	612	2.5
1968	25,959	1,419	5.4	643	2.4
1969	31,013	1,612	5.2	730	2.4
1970	38,199	1,933	5.1	822	2.2

The doubling of Japanese trade with the Soviet Union in 1960 was due to a three-year agreement concluded early that year, providing for a total trade of 440 million dollars during that period (230 million dollars in imports and 210 million dollars in exports)[24] and extending to the Soviet Union the right of deferred payments, a right granted by Japan to her other trading partners and already granted by European nations to the Soviet Union. Deferred payments were to be authorized on a commercial basis by the Export and Import Bank of Japan after a case by case deliberation for export of ships and plants.[25]

Another three-year agreement, signed in February 1963, called for a total trade of between 670 and 700 million dollars in the three years ending in 1965. An agreement was reached also on the development of coastal trade between Japan and the Far Eastern Mari-

24. For the Japanese text of the agreement, signed on 2 March 1960, including the commodity list, see Minshushugi Kenkyukai, ed., *Nihon-Soren koryu nenshi 1960* (Tokyo), pp. 233–38.

25. *Oriental Economist,* April 1960, p. 187. A considerable relaxation in the COCOM list in 1958 and 1959 boosted the export of large freighters. (*Oriental Economist,* January 1959, p. 37.)

time region. Japan was to send such products as cotton textiles, fishing nets, vegetables, canned food, and china, in return for fish products, herbs, marble and vodka.[26]

In 1966 the three-year agreement format was changed to five-years to correspond to the Five Year Plans of the USSR. The agreement concluded on 21 January 1966 did not mention any specific amount, but it was anticipated that the total exports for the years 1966-70 would amount to 1 billion and 100 million dollars and the total imports to 1 billion dollars.[27] As in the period from 1963 to 1966, however, actual trade exceeded expectations and reached almost 3 billion dollars.[28] The major exports specified in the agreement were ships, plants and equipment, steel, chemical products and textiles; imports continued to be confined to raw materials and fuel. The agreement for 1971–75, initialled on 28 April 1971, listed the same commodities indicating the continuation of the same basic trade pattern between the two countries. But the trade estimate for the five-year period exceeded 5 billion dollars, and trade with the USSR was expected nearly to double in the next five years, with a projected annual rate of increase of 12.7 per cent, reflecting Japan's mounting participation in Soviet development of Siberia.[29]

Let us examine the composition of Japan's trade with the USSR from 1958 to 1970,[30] beginning with her imports.

Oil imports started on a small scale in 1958; they became an important item after the 1960 Agreement. From then until 1963 oil occupied nearly 30 per cent of the

26. For details, see *Nihon-Soren koryu nenshi 1963*, pp. 17–19.
27. "Nisso boeki no genjo", in *Chosa geppo,* June 1966, pp. 23–24.
28. *Japan Times,* 29 April 1971.
29. *Ibid.*
30. For a detailed tabulation of Japan's total trade with the USSR and a breakdown by products see Appendix E.

total imports from the Soviet Union, though only 3.4 per cent of Japan's total oil imports or 4.6 per cent, if oil products are included.[31] After 1968, however, the share of oil in Japan's total imports from the USSR declined markedly.

On one hand, Japan was particularly interested in Soviet oil, as the oil from Baku had a lower sulphur content than the oil from the Persian Gulf and thus resulted in a lesser amount of environmental pollution; Japan's expanding economy required ever more fuel, and there seemed to be a rich market for Soviet oil in Japan.[32] On the other hand, a number of factors impeded the natural growth of this trade. The Japanese-owned and Japanese-managed Arabian Oil Company in Kuwait was growing rapidly, and Japan preferred, of course, to rely on her own suppliers than to depend on a foreign source, which could always be cut off. Furthermore, the mammoth tankers built by Japan had reduced transport costs to such an extent that long distances ceased to be an important problem. Although perpetual unrest in the Middle East, from where Japan obtained nearly 90 per cent of her oil, argued in favour of a diversification of her sources of supply, the American, British and Dutch oil companies, which owned a large interest in Japan's refining capacity, resisted purchases of Soviet oil, giving preference to their own. In December 1961, the Defence De-

31. This estimate is based on 1965 figures and mentioned in the report on the energy problems of Japan presented by Dr. Okita Saburo at the second meeting of the Japan-Soviet Economic Committee held in June 1967. (Saburo Okita, *Nihon keizai no vision* (Tokyo, 1968), p. 24.

32. It was projected that by 1975 Japan would be importing 82% of her energy requirements. (Japan, Economic Planning Agency, *New Long Range Economic Plan of Japan [1961–70]: Doubling National Income Plan* [Tokyo, 1961], pp. 90–92; Warren S. Hunsberger, *Japan and USA in World Trade;* Okita, n. 33, pp. 23–24.

partment of the United States announced that it would not purchase jet fuel from Idemitsu Kosan, the largest importer of Soviet oil.[33] Although the United States subsequently relaxed her objections to trade with Communist countries, Japanese imports of oil were limited by the higher freight charges incurred in importing Soviet oil while the Suez canal remained closed.

Furthermore, although Western Siberia, if fully explored, might yield over 3 billion kilolitres of oil,[34] large quantities of Soviet oil could be imported by Japan at competitive rates only if she supplied the USSR with oil exploration equipment and assisted in laying pipelines from the interior to the Pacific Coast.[35] Yet in the early 1960's, the United States put pressure on Japan not to do so.[36]

At the first meeting of the Japan-Soviet Economic Cooperation Committee in March 1966 and repeatedly thereafter, the USSR proposed that Japan grant her long-term credit for the purchase of Japanese equipment and pipes, payment to be made in oil, lumber and pulp.[37] The proposition was of interest in that it held out the assurance of a steady oil supply for many years, but there were misgivings in Japan about extending such large long-term credit to the USSR, particularly since the arrangement might give the latter a handle for exerting political pressure on Japan. With the growth of mutual under-

---

33. Hunsberger, pp. 213–4.

34. Hisaya Shirai "Nisso keizai kyoryoku no kyojitsu," *Asahi Jannaru,* vol. 12, 3 May 1970, pp. 51–52.

35. "Nisso boeki no genjo", pp. 29–30.

36. The United States interfered with Japanese sales of oil pipes to the Soviet Union. (*Nihon-Soren Koryu Nenshi 1963*, pp. 140, 156.)

37. Okita, p. 213; "Nisso boeki no genjo", pp. 29–30; *Oriental Economist,* July 1967, p. 399; Rikuzo Koto "Siberian Development Joint Japanese Soviet Venture," *Asia Scene,* February 1968, pp. 80–83.

standing between the two countries, however, it is reasonable to expect that some sort of Japanese-Soviet collaboration in this area will materialize eventually.

Lumber formed another important item of trade with the Soviet Union. Although lumber from South East Asia and North America accounted for nearly two-thirds of Japan's lumber imports, purchases from the USSR increased annually and were likely to grow rapidly in the future. A basic agreement on the development of forest resources along the Amur River was signed in Tokyo on 29 July 1968 between Kawai Yoshinari of the Komatsu Manufacturing Company and Valery Akkuratov, President of Eksportles. Japan agreed to supply 133 million dollars worth of machinery and facilities, with the USSR paying 20 per cent down and the rest over five years at 5.8 per cent interest, Japan receiving lumber, pulp wood, and wood chips. Japan also was to furnish 30 million dollars worth of consumer goods needed in connection with the project, Soviet payments to be made over 18 months at 5.8 per cent.[38]

Other raw materials and semi-manufactured goods, notably raw cotton and scrap iron, made up the rest of Japan's imports from the USSR. A shortage of medium long-haired cotton in North and Central America made Japan look to the Soviet Union as an alternate source of supply, particularly since the textiles manufactured from this cotton could be exported back to her.[39]

Soviet proposals for supplying electricity to Japan by installing generators in Eastern Siberia and laying power cables under the sea from Sakhalin to Hokkaido and even

38. "Fruition of Japan-Soviet Economic Co-operation," *Asia Scene*, September 1968, pp. 12–13; *Mainichi*, 26 July 1970.

39. Japan, Ministry of International Trade and Industry, *Tsusho Hakusho* (*Kakuron*) *1968*, pp. 195, 623.

transporting electric power to Honshu ran into the twin problems of financing and national security, Japan being reluctant to give the USSR control over part of her electric supply.[40]

Turning to Japanese exports to the Soviet Union, we find that they consisted mostly of manufactured products. Rayon staple, rayon yarn, and tyre cords were included from 1960, and with the relaxation of COCOM restrictions and the introduction of deferred-payment arrangements, ships and factories. In 1962 the Kawai Mission signed a contract in Moscow, selling to the USSR 96 million dollars worth of Japanese ships.[41]

Finding suitable compensation and collateral were major obstacles to Soviet purchases of Japanese factories, as was Soviet reluctance to run up an import surplus. Yet the number of Soviet articles desired by Japan was limited. The problem was partially solved by some companies by importing the products of the factories they built, taking payment, for example, in zinc ore concentrates for the construction of a zinc ore dressing plant.[42] The long-term deferred payments demanded by the Soviet Union ran counter to Japan's cautious policy of limiting deferred payments to five years, and were

40. Dr. Okita ascribed the lack of interest in this proposal to the "island mentality" of the Japanese, who felt that electricity must be produced and consumed in the same country. (Okita, pp. 211–13.) See *The Japan Economic Journal,* 9 September 1969, for the cautious view taken by Japanese companies regarding Soviet proposals.

41. Hunsberger, p. 216. The contract covered 12 tankers of the 35,000 ton deadweight class, 5 freighters of the 12,000 ton class, and 28 other ships, including 10 crane boats. Payment was to be 30 per cent down, with the balance due over 6 years.

42. "New Era in Japan-Soviet Trade," *Oriental Economist,* October 1962, pp. 579–85; "Japan's trade with the Communist Bloc," *Oriental Economist,* April 1964, pp. 218–20; "Trade with USSR and Former Zaibatsu Groups," *Oriental Economist,* July 1964, pp 516–18.

opposed by the United States.[43] With time the attitude of the United States changed and, at any rate, became less influential. But conflicting demands on Japanese credit by various countries and stiff competition by European companies, which also tried to sell the most modern, automated plants to the USSR, remained to be overcome.

The export of manufactures also was hampered by COCOM restrictions and by American limitations on Japan's sharing of technological know-how, acquired through American aid. For example, the export of microwave equipment as well as of a thermo-generating plant for Sakhalin were blocked by licensing arrangements and COCOM regulations; silicone and radar could not even be exhibited at the Moscow Fair on the ground that they were military goods.

The sale of Japanese manufactures to the USSR was inhibited further by the consideration that the latter had not signed the International Patents Treaty and that there was no guarantee, therefore, that Japanese patents would be protected.[44]

The twenty-fold increase in total Japanese-Soviet trade between 1957 and 1970 was furthered by the frank exploration of mutual needs and the exchange of information regarding trade and industry through trade fairs and visits of trade and industrial missions.[45]

The Japanese Industrial Sample Fair, which opened in Moscow in August 1960, was the largest of its kind

43. Stanley D. Metzger, *Law of International Trade*, vol. II, pp. 1147–52.

44. "Soviet Trade, Hopes and Fears," *Oriental Economist*, October 1960, pp. 552–57.

45. For a complete list of the various Japanese Missions which visited the USSR and the Soviet Missions which visited Japan in 1960–63, see *Nihon Soren koryu nenshi*, 1960, pp. 262–347; 1961, pp. 301–84; 1962, pp. 223–317; and 1963, pp. 229–332.

organized by Japan overseas, with big manufacturing industries as well as trading companies represented. It was generously subsidized by the Japanese government and attended by the Minister of International Trade and Industry. A Soviet Trade Fair followed in Tokyo in August 1961.

In 1962, a sixteen member Japanese economic mission, headed by Kawai Yoshinari, president of the Komatsu Manufacturing Industries, visited the Soviet Union to make a preliminary survey of the role Japan might play in the development of Siberia. Soviet plans which were laid out to the mission revealed that the USSR looked upon Japan as a major supplier of the industrial plants and equipment needed for this venture.[46] But while Construction Minister Kono Ichiro was greatly interested in participating in the development of Siberia, Premier Ikeda was not prepared to offer long-term credits to the USSR. Major industries having close ties with the United States also were reluctant at the time to do business with the Communist world.

The situation changed by 1965, when the visits of Nagano Shigeo, president of the Fuji Iron and Steel Company, and Uemura Kogoro, vice chairman of *Keidanren,* to Moscow culminated in the formation of a Japan-Soviet Economic Cooperation Committee, headed by Adachi Tadashi, chairman of the Japan Chamber of Commerce and Industry, and composed of thirty-five top financiers and industrialists. Meeting annually, beginning on 14–25 March 1966, to deal with the various specific problems relating to trade and economic development

46. *Oriental Economist,* July 1962, p. 345; "Nisso boeki no genjo," pp. 579–85.

identified by its subcommittees, the Japan-Soviet Economic Cooperation Committee was to give a fillip to the development of Siberia.[47]

Desirous of attaining economic self-sufficiency for the USSR by the acquisition of modern technology and equipment, Khrushchev had approached President Eisenhower, as soon as the details of the Seven Year Plan for 1959 to 1965 had been worked out, to purchase the equipment of entire plants for the production of consumer goods. American petro-chemical machinery had been desired in particular. But Eisenhower had rejected the Soviet overture, lest the United States build up the economic strength of her political rival,[48] thereby forcing the USSR to turn elsewhere.

The ore, crude petroleum, coal, lumber and wood pulp with which the Soviet Union had wanted to pay for American machinery had not been essential to the United States; they were, however, of great importance to Japan.[49]

Since the United States had done so much to rebuild the Japanese economy and to provide Japan with markets for her goods, the Japanese had long respected American efforts to limit trade with Communist countries. As Japanese competition seriously hurt American manufacturers and Washington put pressure on Tokyo to put "voluntary" restrictions on Japanese exports to the United

47. *Oriental Economist*, May 1966, pp. 263–64.

48. Frank O'Brien, *Crisis in World Communism: Marxism in search of Efficiency* (New York, 1965), pp. 153–70; *East-West Trade Developments*, pp. 1–19, 53–64. *Tenth Battle Act Report*, 1958, pp. 1–19, 53–64.

49. "Soviet Trade with the Free World," in *East-West Trade*, pp. 257–71.

States,[50] as the European Economic Community guarded against the free inflow of cheap Japanese goods,[51] and as the ECAFE region also resorted to import restrictions, Japanese trade with the USSR became increasingly desirable.[52]

The Sino-Soviet split benefitted Japan. Her sale of textile products to the USSR increased,[53] as did her export of heavy machinery to China in exchange for coal, iron ore, salt, soybeans and corn. But although China replaced the Soviet Union as Japan's major Communist trading partner in 1965, by 1967 the USSR regained her old position.[54]

In terms of her total foreign trade, Japan's trade with the Soviet Union still was very small, but its potential

50. Hunsberger, pp. 255–337, 357–63; United States Tariff Commission, *Post War Developments in Japan's Foreign Trade* (Washington, 1958), chapters 5 and 6; "Japanese Exports to the United States," *Fuji Bank Bulletin,* December 1961, pp. 8–21.

51. *Ibid.,* pp. 189, 229–31; United States Economic Commission for Asia and the Far East, *Economic Survey of Asia and the Far East, 1962* (Bangkok, 1963), chapter 4, pp. 119–33; Hisao Kanamori "The European Common Market and Japan's Trade," *The Japan Annual of International Affairs 1962* (Tokyo), pp. 117–27. Japan's fears about Common Market discrimination were shared by the Soviet Union. Michael Kaser, *COMECON, Integration Problem of the Planned Economies* [London, 1967], p. 145.)

52. For a list of the principal Japanese products subject to export restraints, see Hunsberger, p. 236.

53. Textile exports to the Soviet Union occupied the following percentages of total Soviet exports from Japan: 1965: 15.8%; 1966: 22.4%; 1967: 31%; 1968: 32%; 1969: 32%; 1970: 30% ("The Future of Japanese-Soviet Trade," *Asia Scene,* February 1968, p. 89.)

54. Japan's total trade with the Chinese People's Republic amounted to 590 million dollars in 1965; 621 million in 1966; and 558 million in 1967. Japanese trade with the USSR totalled 409 million in 1965; 514 million in 1966; and 610 million in 1967. (*Tsusho hakusho 1968,* pp. 617–27.)

was great, because Japan's rapidly expanding economy was in dire need of raw materials such as lay in Siberia waiting to be exploited.

Adopting a policy of "develop and import," the Japan-Soviet Economic Committee considered plans for such projects as the development of forest resources in the Soviet Far East, the development of copper mines in Udokan and of oil fields in Western Siberia, the laying of pipelines between Western Siberia and Nakhodka, the development of natural gas on Sakhalin, and the expansion of Nakhodka and other Siberian ports.[55]

On 18 December 1970 a contract was signed for the construction of a port at Vrangel to handle coal, lumber chips and freight containers, with the Export Import Bank of Japan funding over a quarter of the project.[56] Construction was begun on a second Trans-Siberian Railway, which was to terminate at Vrangel. Leaving aside the strategic importance of a second Trans-Siberian Railway, safely removed from the Chinese border, it would greatly hasten and cheapen the delivery of Japanese goods to Russia and Europe. Japanese businessmen spoke of super expresses, that would operate at speeds of 200 or 250 kilometres per hour, and cover the distance from the Pacific Ocean to Moscow in two days.[57]

Negotiations for economic cooperation were protracted, as the two sides argued over the proper share of financial participation. In the case of the exploitation of the Udokan copper mines, for example, the USSR wanted Japan to put up 70 per cent of the cost, while

55. *Ibid.*, p. 629; Japan, Cabinet Research Office, *Soren kankei juyo jiko nenshi 1967*, p. 119.

56. *Nihon Keizai*, 19 December 1970; "So-Nichi keizai kankei hatten tojo no atarashi ippo", in Embassy of USSR, *Konnichi no Sorenpo*, 1 February 1971, p. 30.

57. Shirai, pp. 53–54.

the latter was prepared to bear only one fourth of the burden.[58] Occasionally, the Soviets would tie one proposal to another. Knowing that Japan was keen on the development of the natural gas resources of Sakhalin and on the building of a pipeline to carry this gas to Hokkaido, they linked the project with the development of gas resources at Yakutsk and the laying of a pipeline from there to Sakhalin, connecting it with the above-mentioned pipeline to Japan. Tentative agreement was reached on 25 December 1970 for the construction of a gas pipeline from Sakhalin to Hokkaido first and from Yakutsk to Sakhalin later, with Japan to supply pipes sufficiently large to carry both Sakhalin and Yakutsk gas, permitting an eventual annual shipment of 10 billion cubic metres.[59] Discussions were initiated also for the drilling for low-sulphur content petroleum off the shores of the Maritime region, Kamchatka and Sakhalin and for the exploitation of coal resources in the southern part of the Yakut Republic.

Although the USSR and Japan both were vitally interested in the development of Siberia, the ninth Five Year Plan for 1971 to 1975 laid emphasis on the development of Western Siberia, while Japan's aspirations were focused on the Russian Far East. Since the exploitation of the Russian Far East before Western Siberia had been fully developed stood to benefit Japan more than the Soviet Union, the latter felt that Japan should bear a heavier share of the development costs. Furthermore, "joint cooperation" meant different things to the USSR and Japan. The USSR regarded it as a means of obtaining large capital loans at low rates of interest in order to strengthen her economy and improve her bargaining

58. *Asahi*, 16 July 1967; *Tsusho hakusho*, p. 236.
59. *Asahi*, 25 December 1970.

position vis-à-vis China and the United States. Japan saw "joint cooperation" primarily as a means of increasing her exports to the USSR to redress the perennial import surplus in their trade and of securing a nearby supply of natural resources. At the same time, cooperation in Siberia might also improve the prospects of settling territorial and fishery disputes.

Inhibiting factors in the joint development of Siberia[60] included the enormous capital required and the long delay involved before payments in kind could be received. Japan's reluctance to give long-term credits arose from her own financial limitations and priority allotments to South East Asia, whose development and stability were essential in her own national interest. Mistrust of Soviet motives continued and there was fear that economic collaboration with the USSR might be precarious. After Kono's death no one actively lobbied for giving priority to cooperation with the USSR; the tough attitude of the USSR during the annual fishery talks dampened Japanese enthusiasm.

The absence of reliable data regarding the natural resources of Siberia made planning difficult and costly. Preliminary surveys cost money and time. The extremely cold climate of Siberia, the shortage of labour, the complete uninhabitedness of some of the areas to be explored and developed, not to mention the absence of rail and port facilities, compounded the difficulties and costs entailed in the development of the Russian Far East.

The Soviet Union on her part had qualms about possible Japanese entrenchment in Siberia should Japanese economic power be matched again by military power. Yet

60. See David I. Hitchcock Jr. "Joint Development of Siberia: Decision-Making in Japanese-Soviet Relations," *Asian Survey,* vol. 11, no. 3, March 1971, pp. 279–300.

both sides made sincere efforts to surmount the various obstacles. The USSR allowed the stationing of permanent Japanese trade representatives in Moscow and the making of on-the-spot surveys. A Consular Treaty provided for the establishment of Japanese and Soviet consulates at Nakhodka and Sapporo respectively; a subsequent agreement added consular offices in Leningrad and Osaka. A Japan-Soviet Technical Cooperation Agreement was signed on 5 June 1967.[61]

61. *Soren juyo jiko nenshi,* 1967, pp. 119, 121, 127; 1970, p. 195.

4

The Northern Fisheries

As the result of her defeat in the Second World War Japan lost the fishery rights in Russian waters which she had gained after her victory in the Russo-Japanese War and which had been recognized by the Basic Convention of 1925 and perpetuated by the Fishery Convention of 1928 and a series of extensions. The MacArthur Line drawn by SCAP confined Japanese fishing to her coastal waters. The occupation of the Kuriles, Habomai and Shikotan by the Soviet Union and her insistence on a twelve mile territorial limit further restricted Japanese fishing.

Although the San Francisco Peace Treaty provided for the reopening of the northern seas to Japanese fishing, the Soviet Union had not signed the treaty and the representatives of big fishery companies met with the Soviet representative in Tokyo in January 1952 in an attempt to secure Soviet permission.[1] Japanese hopes to continue the talks in Moscow on the occasion of the World Economic

1. "Nisso kosho to suisankai no ugoki," *Chosa geppo,* June 1957, p. 38.

Conference were frustrated by their own government, which refused to let them attend the conference. However, in August 1953, Onishi Kensaku, president of Hokuyo Suisan Company, went to the Soviet Union during a tour of many countries and conferred with officials of the Ministry of Trade. Upon his return, he made a statement to the effect that while the question of normalization was a political problem, his private visit had revealed that trade relations with the USSR could be developed. Though the purpose of his trip as a representative of the fishing circles was not made public, it was believed that he had vainly tried to negotiate the import of fish to be caught by Japanese fishermen in Soviet coastal waters.[2] Combining the trade and fishing questions, the fishery interests continued to agitate for economic relations with the USSR both at meetings of their own and at the meetings of the Association for Promotion of Trade with the Soviet Union and China (*Chu So Boeki Sokushin Kaigi*). Hiratsuka Tsunejiro of the Greater Japan Fisheries Society (*Dai Nihon Suisan Kai*) aired Japan's grievances about fishing in northern waters at the World Peace Conferences at Berlin and Stockholm during May-June 1954 and called for the convening of a World Fisheries Conference. In a pamphlet which he distributed at the peace conferences, Hiratsuka advocated mutual understanding with the Soviet Union and a more positive approach towards normalization. His representative, Fukunaga Kazuomi, arrived in Moscow on 10 August to plead for the right of Japanese fishing vessels to operate in Soviet coastal waters.[3]

Fukunaga had been preceded on 21 July by a group of seven Diet members, who also had attended the World

2. *Ibid.*
3. *Ibid.*, p. 39.

Peace Conferences. Foreign Minister Andrei Vyshinsky, with whom they met, proposed that cultural exchange and regular trade could be established prior to the signing of a peace treaty. He followed a softer line on aiding Japanese vessels in distress between Hokkaido and Habomai and, while clinging to the twelve mile limit, agreed that fishing beyond that line should be free. He even went along with the idea of a joint study of fishery problems. But he made it clear that no expansion of Japanese fishery rights could take place without a proper official agreement between the two governments following normalization.[4] Fukunaga was told the same by the secretary of the Soviet Ministry of Fisheries.[5] Hirano Yoshitaro, a member of the Nemuro City Peace Promotion and Economic Promotion Committee, learned from his counterpart on the Soviet Peace Promotion Committee on 28 August that the Soviet Union was prepared not only to relight the lighthouse in Kaigarajima near Nemuro and give relief to Japanese ships in distress but to conclude a fisheries agreement, if the Japanese government would initiate negotiations.[6]

As noted, the Hatoyama cabinet, which took office in December 1954, was favourably inclined toward normalization of relations with the USSR. The fact that Dominitsky gained access to Hatoyama through Kuhara Fusanosuke, president of the National Council of Associations for the Normalization of Relations with the Soviet Union and China, was no coincidence; the fishery interests worked through this council to get the Soviet representative and the Japanese government together.

The appointment of Kono Ichiro, who was closely

4. *Sovieto nenpo*, 1955, p. 667.
5. "Nisso kosho to suisankai no ugoki," p. 40.
6. *Ibid.*

associated with Hiratsuka, as minister of agriculture and forestry was a boon for the fisheries interests, which obtained an increase in the number of fleets allowed to operate in northern waters, permits being given to fleets of the *Taiyo, Nissui* and *Nichiro* fisheries.[7] But an arrangement made between fishery representatives and Soviet officials for the exchange of teams of specialists to study each other's fishing failed to materialize when the Japanese government refused to issue the required visas.[8]

The increase in Japanese fishing operations worried the USSR, because of a decline in salmon stock in the North Pacific. At the United Nations Conference for Conservation of the Living Resources of the Sea, held in Rome between 18 April and 16 May 1955, the Soviet delegate linked the decrease of pink salmon in the Far East to the resumption of Japanese fishing in the northern seas.[9] The same unsubstantiated charge was repeated by the USSR on 10 February 1956 in announcing that the Soviet Council of Ministers was concerned about the depletion of salmon and trout resources by reckless Japanese fishing.[10] The Japanese Department of Fisheries denied that Japanese fishing fleets were guilty of reckless practices, pointing out that their annual catch totalled less than 60 per cent of prewar levels. The Greater Japan Fisheries Society contended that the decline in the number of fish

7. For details see Zengo Ohira, "Dai niji taisen ato ni okeru Nisso gyogyo kankei," *Kokusaiho gaiko zasshi,* March 1962, pp. 277–316; "Nisso gyogyo kosho to suisankai," *Nihon keizai no ugoki,* July 1956, pp. 67–74.

8. "Nisso kosho to suisankai no ugoki," pp. 43–44, 49.

9. *Report of the International Technical Conference on the Conservation of Living Resources of the Sea,* 18 April to 16 May 1955 at Rome, UN General Assembly A/Conf, 10/5 Rev. 2, A/Conf. 10/6 of June 1955; Norin Keizai Kenkyujo, *Hokuyo gyogyo soran* (Tokyo, 1960) pp. 78–82.

10. *Pravda,* 11 February 1956, in *CDSP,* vol. 8, no. 6, pp. 33–34.

coming to lay eggs in the river beds was due not to reckless fishing by Japanese, but due to the Soviet development of river basins and the consequent loss of river beds for the laying of eggs. The fisheries industry concurred with the need for the conservation of resources, but felt that joint study and deliberation were required to find an equitable solution.[11] The Soviet government, however, was unwilling to delay the matter, and in a radio broadcast on 21 March 1956 limited Japanese fishing beyond what became commonly known as the Bulganin Line.[12]

Canada and the United States too had complained that the Japanese method of fishing, with small vessels operating from a mother ship, provided excessive catches, and in 1951 Japan had agreed to abstain from fishing in the North Pacific, east of longitude 175°.[13] The Special Committee on Japanese-Soviet Fisheries (*Nisso gyogyo tokubetsu iinkai*), formed by the Japanese companies upon the commencement of talks with the USSR, was willing to assist in conservation measures.[14] It was the unilateral nature of the Soviet decision that aroused the resentment of the fisheries people both against the Soviet government and against their own, which had contributed to the rigidity of the Soviet stand by bungling the negotiations. Angered, they threatened to sail in defiance of the Soviet decree and leave their protection up to the Japa-

11. "Nisso kosho to suisankai no ugoki," pp. 45–46.
12. The fish conservation zone encompassed the entire Okhotsk Sea and the western part of the Bering Sea and the Pacific Ocean adjacent to the territorial waters of the USSR, to the west and northwest of a conventional line running from Cape Olyutorsky in the Bering Sea south along the meridian to point 48° north 170° 25′ east, thence southwest until it reached the limits of the territorial waters of the USSR at Anuchin island in the lesser Kuriles. (*Pravda*, 21 March 1956 in *CDSP*, vol. 8 no. 10, p. 30.)
13. "Nisso gyogyo kosho to suisan kai," no. 7. pp. 68–69.
14. "Nisso kosho to suisankai no ukogi," p. 42.

nese government, but the folly of such a move was made clear by the publication of the Soviet decision on 21 April 1956, which detailed the penalties that violators would face, and by the warning of Dominitsky that vessels venturing beyond the Bulganin Line would be seized without fail.[15]

The unilateral nature of the Soviet decision and its timing brought home to the Japanese the disadvantage of not having normal relations with the USSR. In order to facilitate the normalization of relations, the fishery industry urged the separation of the fishery issue from the territorial problem and the restoration of relations on the basis of a fishery agreement only.

The fishery industry prevailed upon the government to include three fishery representatives in the delegation that was to proceed to Moscow: Nakabe Kenkichi, president of *Taiyo,* Suzuki Kyutei, president of *Nihon Suisan,* and Fujita Iwao, vice-president of *Dai Nihon Suisan Kai.* Although Kono declared that the delegation could deal only with the fisheries questions,[16] the fishery people countered that no useful fisheries agreement could be attained unless the early termination of the state of war and the opening of diplomatic relations could be negotiated also, with the territorial problem being left for later.[17]

Before the delegation's departure Fujita Iwao conferred with Dominitsky. As the delegation was on its way to the USSR, Ambassador Malik handed to Ambassador Nishi Haruhiko in London a note asking that Dominitsky be allowed to leave Japan to assist in the Moscow talks and that another Soviet official be allowed to enter Japan

15. *Ibid.,* pp. 47–49; *Asahi* (evening), 9 April 1956; *Izvestiya,* 21 April 1956 in *CDSP,* vol. 8, no. 16, p. 21; "Northern Fisheries," in *Asahi,* 16 and 17 April 1956.

16. Kono Ichiro, *Ima dakara hanaso* (Tokyo, 1958), p. 9.

17. *Tokyo,* 11 April 1956; *Sankei,* 24 April 1956.

to replace him. Two or three additional Soviet officials should be given entry permits to Japan to handle the problems arising out of the fishery negotiations. Alarmed that the Soviet Union might be trying to legitimize the status of her mission and seek to normalize diplomatic relations by installments, Foreign Minister Shigemitsu gave consideration to recalling the Kono Mission and denying an exit visa to Dominitsky, but upon further reflection went along with the plans, allowing, however, the entry of only one person in place of Dominitsky and specifying that he would not be given diplomatic status and privileges and would be treated merely as an official responsible for dealing with fishery problems.[18]

The northern fisheries talks were held in Moscow from 28 April to 14 May. The Soviet delegation was headed by A. A. Ishkov, Minister of Fisheries. Sub-committees worked out specific issues, then submitted them for approval by the general meeting. By 11 May agreement was reached on a draft convention concerning high seas fishery in the North Pacific and a draft agreement for cooperation in the rescue of persons in distress at sea. When the agreement was about to be signed the following day, however, Ishkov put forth the condition that the agreement allotting to Japan for 1956 a catch of 65,000 tons within the Bulganin Line be valid only if the fisheries convention went into effect. (This could happen only, Bulganin had told Kono on 9 May, if the relations between their countries were normalized.) Kono protested to Ishkov, and Ishkov, after consulting with Bulganin, yielded. But while the agreement regarding

18. Sergei Chivinsky, third secretary in the London Embassy, took Dominitsky's place. He arrived on 13 May 1956. Later two more officials were allowed to come to deal with the question of fishing permits. (*Sovieto nenpo 1958*, pp. 374–75; *Hokuyo gyogyo soran*, p. 82.

fishing in the northern waters was signed on 14 May without discussing the validity of the convention, the Soviet Union affixed her signature with the express understanding that the negotiations for the normalization of relations would be resumed shortly. A joint communiqué stated that Kono and Ishkov had exchanged views on normalization and had agreed on the resumption of talks for this purpose not later than 31 July 1956.[19]

The fishing operations in 1956 were less successful than expected, because of delays in the receipt of the necessary permits. An attempt by the Department of Fisheries to obtain permission for the extension of the fishing period was rebuffed by the Soviets.[20] Again the importance of being on better terms with the USSR was impressed on the fishery circles and they pressed for the restoration of diplomatic relations.

The ratification of the Joint Convention in December 1956 brought the High Seas Fisheries Convention into effect. In accordance with Article 3 of the convention there was established a Northwest Pacific Fisheries Commission, composed of three Japanese and three Soviet members, which met annually to determine the yearly catch of salmon, herring and crabs and to make recommendations regarding conservation and the increase of fishery resources. Held alternately in Tokyo and Moscow, the meetings of the commission became known as the

---

19. *Sovieto nenpo 1958*, p. 374; Shunichi Matsumoto, *Moscow ni kakeru niji* (Tokyo, 1966), pp. 99–101. For the text of the convention regarding fisheries and the agreement for the rescue of persons in distress at sea, see *The Japanese Annual of International Law*, 1957, pp. 119–27.

20. The Soviet representative also delayed matters in issuing permits. An attempt was thus made to force Japan's hand to grant proper diplomatic status to the Soviet represenative. (*Hokuyo gyogyo soran*, p. 89.)

"100 day meetings" because of their length.[21] The wrangling that ensued every February over the size of the catch, as the Japanese disputed Soviet depletion claims, was usually brought to a halt by the realization that further disputation would fatally delay the departure of the fishing fleets. In the discussions the Japanese were at an unavoidable disadvantage, because the fishing on the high seas of the convention area was done exclusively by their vessels; the Soviets confined themselves to the rivers within the USSR. The regulations thus applied only to the Japanese, and while the commission was informed of estimated annual river catches, it had no authority over them.

Four topics overshadowed the annual fishery talks: (1) the extension of areas where fishing for salmon and eventually crab was prohibited; (2) the maximum annual catch; (3) the duration of the fishing season; and (4) the length of the drift-nets, the distance between them, and the size of their meshes.

At the very first session in 1957, the commission decided to prohibit salmon fishing within 20 miles of the coast in the waters south of latitude 40°N and within 40 miles of the coast in other areas. In 1958 the areas were revised by drawing straight lines between the various points even though the coastline was uneven. In 1959 they were substantially extended to the areas southeast of the Kamchatka peninsula and around the Komondorskiye Islands. In 1960 and again in 1961 two more areas south of latitude 48°N were closed to salmon fishing.[22]

21. The meetings actually lasted anywhere from 28 days in 1969 to 122 days in 1959. *Chosa geppo,* June 1966, p. 37; *Soren kandei juyo jiko nenshi,* 1967, 1968, 1969, 1970.

22. *Sovieto nenpo 1958,* pp. 375–76; *Sovieto nenpo 1959,* p. 367; *Nihon Soren koryu nenshi, 1960,* pp. 229–32; *1961,* pp. 261–64.

Japanese protests were to no avail, even though Foreign Minister Kishi and Agriculture Minister Kono intervened. Using the question of the total catch as a bargaining weapon, the Soviets obtained Kono's agreement to the closing of the Sea of Okhotsk to salmon fishing from 1 January 1959.[23]

The closing by the USSR of Peter the Great Bay to all foreign vessels and airplanes on 20 July 1957 was another great blow to the Japanese fishery industry. Since the closing of the more than 100 nautical mile wide entrance to the bay was contrary to international law, the United States and Great Britain as well as Japan protested, but the Soviet Union did not budge, as she was determined to maintain maximum security in the approaches to Vladivostok.[24]

In 1961 the Soviets proposed the application of the regulations of the northern fisheries convention to salmon fishing throughout the Pacific, for they felt that the Japanese catch in the areas south of latitude 45°N had increased to such an extent since the signing of the convention that it was nullifying its objective. The Japanese strongly objected not only because they thought they were taking adequate conservation measures, but also because they did not want to fall under Soviet supervision in areas south of latitude 45°N as well. To meet Soviet criticism, Japan voluntarily reduced her catch for 1961 by 20,000 tons compared to that of 1959 and implemented the system of permit fishing in those waters.[25]

23. For Soviet justification for closing the Okhotsk Sea to fishing, see *CDSP*, vol. 10, no. 7, pp. 22–23.

24. Notes verbale exchanged between Japan and the Soviet Union, in *The Japanese Annual of International Law, 1958*, pp. 213–8; Zengo Ohira, "Fishing Problems between Soviet Russia and Japan," *ibid.*, pp. 13–18.

25. *Nihon Soren koryu nenshi 1961*, pp. 261–64; *Oriental Econo-*

In 1961, when Premier Mikoyan visited Japan in connection with the industrial fair, Kono got his consent for
the holding of preliminary meetings by experts in November. Beginning with the 1962 session of the commission,
therefore, the annual negotiations began more smoothly.
Yet the Soviet side persisted in the demand that the convention be applied also to the region south of latitude
45°N.[26] Japan finally consented in 1962 with the understanding that the regulations would be more lenient in
the south and would not be enforced by Soviet patrol
boats; competent Soviet officials were placed aboard
Japanese ships.[27] Some areas west of Kamchatka were
closed to crab fishing and the amount of crab fishing
elsewhere was regulated by the commission.[28]

Crab fishing became a source of dispute in 1964, when
the international Convention on the Continental Shelf
became operative upon ratification by 22 states. Since
the convention recognized that coastal states had
sovereign rights over the natural resources of the continental shelf, the Soviet Union, which had ratified the convention, declared that crabs were a natural resource of
the continental shelf and their exploitation her own
sovereign right, Japan being able to crab only as, when,
and where she permitted. Japan, which had not ratified

---

mist, May 1962, p. 259. For Soviet criticism about Japanese violations of the convention, see *Pravda,* 18 March 1959, in *CDSP,* vol.
11, no. 11, p. 24; *Izvestiya,* 28 March 1959, in *CDSP,* vol. 11, no.
13, pp. 20–21; *Izvestiya,* 3 December 1960, in *CDSP,* vol. 12, no.
49, pp. 22–23.

26. *Nihon Soren koryu nenshi,* 1962, pp. 29–30.

27. *Nihon Soren koryu nenshi,* 1962, pp. 32–34; *Oriental Economist,* June 1962, p. 339.

28. The annual catch of crabs was limited as follows (in 1000
boxes): For the Soviet Union 480 in 1958; 420 in 1959; 390 in
1960; 278 in 1962 and again in 1963. For Japan 320 in 1958; 280
in 1959; 260 in 1960 and in 1961, 252 in 1962 and in 1963.

the convention, disputed that crabs were a natural resource of the continental shelf. The fact that the Soviet
Union herself had in 1965 signed an agreement with
the United States limiting Russian crabbing in American
waters made her feel fully justified in increasing her quota
in her own region.[29] In 1969 the crab negotiations were
separated from the main negotiations and were to be
held every March in Moscow.[30]

Restrictions on herring fishing were also introduced
and the catching of roe-bearing herring banned completely in the Sea of Okhotsk.[31]

The maximum annual catch of salmon was the subject of repeated controversy. The Soviet side tried to cling
to the agreement made by Kono and Ishkov during the
Moscow fishery negotiations that fishing north of latitude
45°N would be limited to 100,000 tons during rich haul
years and 80,000 tons during lean haul years; Japan
wanted a higher amount, contending that the estimates
had not been based on scientific surveys.

The actual number of tons of salmon caught by the
Japanese in zone A (north of latitude 45°N) amounted
to 121,094 in 1957; 110,100 in 1958; 85,100 in 1959;
66,606 in 1960; 64,928 in 1961; 54,512 in 1962; 56,616
in 1963; 54,561 in 1964; 56,000 in 1965; and 48,000 in
1966. In zone B (south of latitude 45°N) they caught
60,445 in 1957; 86,400 in 1958; 94,100 in 1959; 80,200

29. For the text of the international convention see *American
Journal of International Law,* vol. 52, 1958, pp. 858–62. The text
of the Soviet-American agreement is in *International Legal Materials,*
vol. 4, March 1965, pp. 359–61. For the Soviet-Japanese dispute on
crab fishing at the 1968 meeting, see "Kiro ni tatsu Nisso gyogyo,"
in *Asahi,* 27 April 1968.

30. *Asahi,* 2 May 1971; "Japan-Soviet Crab Talks," in *Japan
Times,* 1 May 1971.

31. *Ibid.*

in 1960; 91,430 in 1961; 41,142 in 1962; 63,779 in 1963; 45,895 in 1964; 59,000 in 1965; and 48,000 in 1966.[32] Japanese tonnage limits in both zones together totalled 108,000 in 1967; 93,000 in 1968; 105,000 in 1969; 90,000 in 1970 and 95,000 in 1971.[33] In comparison, the Soviets caught 120,000 tons in 1958; 94,100 in 1959; 69,500 in 1960; 79,700 in 1961; 60,560 in 1962; 81,100 in 1963; 47,715 in 1964; 85,000 in 1965; and 50,000 in 1966.[34]

The duration of the fishing season was a subject of controversy, because the Russians wanted it to end by 15 or 25 July on the ground that there was likely to be a large number of baby salmon in the waters by August. But the Japanese prevailed, and fishing continued until 10 August, as specified in the convention. No specific date for the beginning of the fishing season had been set by the convention and there was room for manoeuvre, though as the negotiations dragged out every year the actual departure of the fishing fleets often was delayed.[35]

The regulations regarding the length of the drift nets and the width of the mesh were reconsidered from time to time and modifications made in order to regulate the amount of fish caught per ship and to prevent the catch of very small fish.

In accordance with the convention, scholars and fisheries experts were exchanged to study the conservation of fishing resources. The first exchange took place in 1958. In 1961, a committee of experts spent a whole month in Moscow evaluating the various kinds of fishery re-

32. *Nihon-Soren koryu nenshi,* 1960, 1961, 1962, 1963; *Chosa geppo,* June 1966, p. 38.

33. *Soren juyo jiko nenshi,* 1968–70; *Asahi* 2 May 1971.

34. *Nihon-Soren koryu nenshi,* 1960, 1961, 1962, 1963; Japan, *Chosa geppo,* June 1966, p. 38.

35. *Nihon Soren koryu nenshi,* 1962, p. 34.

sources. In 1962 and 1963 Soviet investigation teams visited Japan. In 1963 an accord was reached between the experts of the Greater Japan Fisheries Society and the experts of the USSR regarding a salmon hatching programme, and a protocol on this subject was signed.[36]

In the field of fisheries, therefore, Japanese-Soviet relations developed to a stage where they were based on joint consultation and yielded fruitful results. The gradual decrease in the amount of fish caught showed that Soviet fears of the depletion of salmon, though perhaps exaggerated, were not groundless. The Soviet Union had not been the first state to accuse Japan of reckless fishing, nor had she been alone in imposing restrictions on fishing on the high seas as a means of conservation.

Scientifically motivated as Soviet fishery measures may have been, however, they had their political use. The need for Soviet goodwill and cooperation to assure smooth fishing was a powerful persuader for obtaining amicable Japanese relations with the USSR. On the other hand, Soviet restrictions could be used by nationalists in Japan to inflame public opinion against the USSR. In this respect the denial of the coastal waters of Habomai, Shikotan and the Kurile Islands to Japanese exploitation remained a festering sore.

36. *Sovieto nenpo 1959*, pp. 367–8; *Nihon Soren koryu nenshi*, 1960, pp. 116, 166; 1961, pp. 18, 140; 1962, p. 305; 1963, p. 321.

5

The Northern Territories

The Joint Declaration normalizing relations between Japan and the USSR provided for the return of Habomai and Shikotan after the conclusion of a peace treaty. No mention was made of the Southern Kurile Islands, whose return Japan was demanding with mounting tenacity.

As noted, with the outbreak of the Cold War the United States had bolstered the Japanese position. When Japan, in the summer of 1955, had inquired of the major powers that had signed the San Francisco Peace Treaty whether (1) clause 8 of the Potsdam Declaration (stipulating that Japanese sovereignty should be limited to Honshu, Hokkaido, Kyushu, Shikoku and such minor islands as they would determine) referred to the Yalta Agreement and whether (2) the Soviet Union could unilaterally claim South Sakhalin and the Kuriles as her territory under this clause, the United States had replied that the Yalta Agreement was merely a statement of Allied purpose and had no final validity.

The United States had contended that, as no mention had been made of the Yalta Agreement in the Potsdam

Declaration which Japan had accepted, the Yalta Agreement was not binding on Japan. Having preceded the Potsdam Declaration, the Yalta Agreement could not be meant by clause 8 of the Potsdam Declaration. Besides, as the Potsdam Declaration had specified that the final territorial limits of Japan would be decided after consideration by the countries which joined in the Potsdam Declaration, no unilateral decision by the USSR was possible. Neither SCAPIN 677 nor Clause 2 of the San Francisco Treaty had made a final disposition of South Sakhalin and the Kuriles; their ultimate disposition must be settled by international agreement. As for Habomai and Shikotan, they were historically and legally part of Hokkaido.

The United Kingdom had concurred informally that the Yalta Agreement had not been specified in clause 8 of the Potsdam Declaration and that the Soviet Union could not unilaterally take possession of the territories in question. France had responded that the Potsdam Declaration and the Cairo and Yalta Agreements had been merely indications of Allied intent and in order to have validity under international law would have to be confirmed by either a peace treaty or a joint declaration on terms of complete equality.[1]

In October 1955 Japan had sent two more queries to the Western powers: (1) Had the leaders who participated in the Yalta Conference been aware, when using the term "Kurile Islands", that Kunashiri and Etorofu, which were very close to Hokkaido, were Japanese territory occupied only by Japanese and had never passed into foreign hands and had they taken into consideration the fact that in the treaty concluded between Japan and

1. Shunichi Matsumoto, *Moscow ni kakeru niji* (Tokyo, 1966), pp. 60–62.

Russia in 1875 only the 18 islands north of Uruppu had been included in the definition of the "Kurile Islands," not Kunashiri and Etorofu?[2] (2) Did the United States, which had played the major role in the formulation of the San Francisco Peace Treaty, acknowledge that the mention of "Kurile Islands" in article 2 (c) of the treaty did not include Kunashiri and Etorofu?

The State Department had replied that the Yalta Agreement had dealt neither with the geographical limits nor the historical position of the Kuriles; it had not conceded the territories and had no validity. There was no record to show that the signatories of the Yalta Agreement had intended to give to the Soviet Union territory which had not formerly belonged to Russia. No definition had been made of the Kurile Islands either in the Peace Treaty with Japan or in the minutes of the San Francisco Conference. In the opinion of the United States, therefore, any dispute over the meaning of "Kurile Islands" should be referred to the International Court of Justice, as specified in article 22 of the San Francisco Treaty. If this was not feasible in the present circumstances, the United States would have no objection to Japanese attainment of the restoration of Kunashiri and Etorofu by direct negotiation with the USSR, either by convincing her that they did not form part of the Kurile Islands or by relinquishing in a peace treaty with the USSR all rights to the Kuriles and South Sakhalin in exchange for Soviet return of Kunashiri and Etorofu.

The United Kingdom and France had not entirely agreed with the American position, especially on the "intention" of the Yalta Agreement. France had pointed out that while article 2 (c) of the San Francisco Peace

2. For a refutation of this argument, see G. A. Lensen, *The Strange Neutrality* (Tallahassee, 1972), p. 218, note o.

Treaty specified only the Kuriles, reference was made to the Southern Kuriles in the minutes of the conference. The Japanese representative at the conference himself had referred to Kunashiri and Etorofu as Southern Kuriles. France had noted, furthermore, that referral to the International Court of Justice was binding only in the case of disputes between signatories of the San Francisco Treaty; it was not binding in disputes that arose between a signatory and a nonsignatory.[3]

On 7 September 1956, as related above, the United States had publicly come out in support of Japanese claims to Kunashiri and Etorofu.[4]

While the Joint Declaration did not provide for future negotiations regarding the territorial issue, Japan argued that even though no specific mention had been made in the declaration, it had been the intention of the signatories that the territorial issue would be negotiated in connection with a peace treaty. Her argument was based on the fact that the Soviet Union had allowed the publication of the Matsumoto-Gromyko correspondence, which stated clearly that the Soviet Union was prepared to consider a peace treaty, including the territorial question, after diplomatic relations were restored.

As seen, however, Khrushchev had felt that the territorial issue should be deemed settled with the return of Habomai and Shikotan, and the Soviet Union did not regard the publication of Gromyko's letter to Matsumoto as a definite commitment on her part.

When the Japanese government in June 1957 sought to discuss the problem of fishing in Russian territorial waters around Sakhalin and the Kuriles, the USSR agreed, but

3. Matsumoto, pp. 62–64.
4. Japan, Ministry of Foreign Affairs, Public Information Bureau, *Hoppo ryodo* (Tokyo, December 1961), p. 14; *DSB*, 24 September 1956, p. 484.

in February-March 1958 tied the issue to the conclusion of a peace treaty and would not consider it separately.[5] On his visit to Japan on 27 August 1958, Ishkov reiterated that an early solution of the problem of fishing in Soviet territorial waters could be achieved if Japan took steps for concluding a peace treaty.[6] The Kishi administration was not prepared, however, to sign away Japanese rights to the Southern Kuriles in exchange for a few fishing grounds and Habomai and Shikotan and decided to wait with a peace treaty.

With the conclusion of the Revised Security Treaty between Japan and the United States, the USSR stiffened her position. In a memorandum handed to Ambassador Kadowaki Suemitsu on 27 January 1969, she declared that since the new military treaty was directed against her and against the Chinese People's Republic, she could not contribute to extending the territory available for foreign troops by turning Habomai and Shikotan over to Japan and would transfer them only on the condition that all foreign troops were withdrawn from Japan and a peace treaty signed between the USSR and Japan.[7]

The commander of the Soviet Far Eastern Military District had warned in an article in *Pravda* on 20 January 1960 that if Japan became involved in military plans against the USSR, the Soviet people would find it difficult to understand why Habomai and Shikotan should be handed over to her, as they could be immediately used by foreign armed forces,[8] but the Foreign Office had not taken the threat seriously.[9] As the Soviet Union went

5. *Sovieto nenpo*, 1959, pp. 365–66; *Pravda*, 23 March 1958, in *CDSP*, vol. 10, no. 12, p. 26.
6. *Asahi*, 28 August 1958.
7. *Pravda*, 29 January 1960, in *CDSP*, vol. 12, no. 4, pp. 19–20.
8. *CDSP*, vol. 12, no. 3, pp. 26–27.
9. *Japan Times*, 22 January 1960.

back on the promise made in the Joint Declaration by imposing a new condition, the watch and wait policy of Japan regarding the northern territorial issue was discredited. Japanese protests that the Soviet action constituted interfence in Japan's domestic affairs and was a violation of the Joint Declaration brought no results.[10]

When Mikoyan visited Tokyo in August 1961 in order to inaugurate the Soviet Industrial Fair, he brought Premier Ikeda a letter from Khrushchev, stating that the Soviet government was prepared to consider any problems existing between their countries in order to put Japanese-Soviet relations on a better footing. Ikeda wrote in reply that the existence of the Security Pact with the United States and the presence of American bases in Japan were no obstacles to the conclusion of a Japanese-Soviet peace treaty, because such a defence agreement had been in effect at the time of the signing of the Joint Declaration and the declaration had recognized the right of Japan to enter into any regional alliance. It was the refusal of the Soviet Union to return Japanese territory that stood in the way of a peace treaty.

In the correspondence which ensued both sides reiterated the familiar arguments; the Soviet Union insisted that the territorial question had been settled by the international agreements, Japan claimed that they were subject to negotiation.[11] As Khrushchev made plain to a visiting Japanese parliamentary delegation in September 1964, he was reluctant to return even Habomai and Shikotan until the Americans pulled out of Japan.[12]

10. For the entire correspondence between Japan and the Soviet Union on this issue from January to July 1960, see *Nihon Soren koryu nenshi*, 1960, pp. 216–28.

11. For the full text of the correspondence between Ikeda and Khrushchev, see *Nihon Soren koryu nenshi 1961*, pp. 271–85.

12. *Pravda*, 20 September 1964, in *CDSP*, vol. 16, no. 38, pp. 3–6.

The Japanese lure of economic collaboration if the territorial question was settled amicably[13] was not swallowed by the Russians who charged that unfounded claims were being advanced to prevent better relations with the Soviet Union. When the Japanese government announced in 1969 that henceforth Kunashiri, Etorofu, Habomai and Shikotan would be shown on Japanese maps as Japanese territory, *Izvestiya* accused it of reviving Japan's "old Asia policy."[14]

Foreign Minister Aichi Kiichi, who visited Moscow in September 1969 on his way to Washington to discuss the reversion of Okinawa, failed to move the Russians, who feared that the revision of national boundaries established during the Second World War in one place, might revive territorial issues elsewhere.[15] The conclusion of a treaty between the USSR and the Federal Republic of Germany on 12 August 1970, in which both nations mutually renounced any territorial claims,[16] added weight to the Soviet argument that the acceptance of boundaries decided as the result of World War II would contribute to the improvement of relations in Asia as well.[17]

13. Hints were made to this effect by Foreign Minister Shiina Etatsuburo on his visit to Moscow in January 1966 and by Foreign Minister Miki Takeo on his visit to Moscow in July 1967. They were repeated by Miki in his talks with Baibakov, head of GOSPLAN, when the latter was in Tokyo in January 1968. (*Asian Almanac,* pp. 1442–1443, 2252, 2609). Foreign Minister Aichi Kiichi declared in his foreign policy statement to the Diet in January 1971 that "the unsolved territorial issue is a major obstacle in the development of relations." (*Japan Times,* 23 January 1971.)

14. V. Kudryavtsev, "At the Crossroads," *Izvestiya,* 26 June 1969, in *CDSP,* vol. 21, no. 26.

15. Japan, Ministry of Foreign Affairs, *The Northern Territorial Issue* (Tokyo, 1970), p. 23.

16. *Pravda,* 13 August 1970, in *CDSP,* vol. 22, no. 33, pp. 2–3.

17. *Pravda,* 29 August 1970, and Moscow broadcasts of 5 September 1970, 30 September 1970, and 18 October 1970, in *Soren kankei juyo jiko nenshi,* 1970, pp. 185, 187, 189, 190.

The Japanese government, on the other hand, stepped up its campaign for the reversion of the northern territories when the United States agreed to return Okinawa and whipped up public support at home.[18] When Premier Sato, in a speech at the United Nations General Assembly in September 1970, sought to arouse international public opinion as well, the Soviet government protested against this as an unfriendly act.[19]

18. Advertising towers, about six metres high, were erected by the Northern Territories Issue Research Organization, subsidized by government funds at Yaesuguchi, Tokyo, and two other places with the inscription "Demand the return of the Northern Territories that belonged to our fathers." (Minoru Shimuzu, "Japan Soviet Relations," *Japan Times Weekly*, 15 May 1971.

19. *Soren kankei juyo jiko nenshi*, 1970, p. 191.

6

Political Normalization

The Soviet Union was less interested in the American withdrawal from Okinawa, in the East China Sea, than from Japan proper, whence American bombers could easily reach her. When Soviet attacks on the Security Pact and on Japanese cooperation with the United States proved counterproductive,[1] Moscow changed tactics and began advocating a policy of neutrality for Japan.

In a note, handed by Gromyko to Ambassador Kadowaki Suemitsu on 2 December 1958, the Soviet government asserted that Japanese independence and security could be insured best by the country's rejection of rearmament and war, a policy that would be consonant

---

1. D. Vasilyev, "Washington Regime for Japan," *New Times*, 5 September 1957, pp. 10–12; *Pravda*, 7 September 1957, in *Sovieto nenpo*, 1959, p. 364; *New Times*, 5 December 1957, p. 17; V. Kudrayavesev, "Down the Old Corrupt Road," *Izvestiya*, 23 October 1958, in *CDSP*, vol. 10, no. 43, pp. 14–15. For the text of notes exchanged between the Soviet Union and Japan on this question in May-June 1958, see *Pravda*, 20 June 1958, in *CDSP*, vol. 10, no. 25, p. 16. See also Nikkan Rodo Sha, *Nisso kan juyo kokan bunsho* (Tokyo 1964), p. 43; and *Sovieto nenpo*, 1959, pp. 384–85.

with the Japanese Constitution. The Japanese government replied that its alignment with the "Free World"
did not prevent the maintenance of friendly relations
with the Socialist World, but that the suggestion constituted Soviet interference in Japanese foreign policy
and as such could not promote friendly relations between the two countries. Yet the call to neutralism struck
a responsive cord among the Japanese public and Khrushchev reiterated in a speech on 27 January 1959 the need
for creating "a zone of peace, above all, an atom-free
zone in the Far East and the entire Pacific Basin."[2] In his
replies to the questionnaire by the Japanese Press Service
on 20 April 1959, Khrushchev contended that a neutralist
policy would strengthen Japan's independence, exalt her
status in international society, and would help to relieve
tension in the Far East and contribute to world peace. He
added that if Japan adopted such a policy, those clauses
in the Sino-Soviet Treaty of 1950 which were directed
against her, would be modified.[3]

Ambassador Nikolai Fedorenko in a speech before
the *Nisso Shinzen Kyokai* on 25 January 1959 declared
that there were no conflicting interests dividing Japan and
the Soviet Union. Their differing ideologies did not prevent the development of friendly relations. It was the hope
of his country, he echoed, that Japan would pursue a
policy of neutrality in the interests of world peace.[4]

The Japanese Communist Party supported the Soviet
call for neutrality,[5] although heretofore it had worked

2. *Pravda*, 28 January 1959, in *CDSP*, vol. 11, no. 4, p. 20.

3. *Nisso kan juyo kokan bunsho*, no. 26, pp. 265–70; D.
Vasilyev, "Policy Which Meets the Interests of the Japanese
People," *Izvestiya*, 3 May 1959, in *CDSP*, vol. 10, no. 18, pp. 22–23.

4. "Soren no tai-nichi churitsuka seisaku," *Chosa geppo*, February 1960, pp. 21–23.

5. *Akahata*, 19 January 1959.

against it, advocating outright opposition to the "imperialists."[6]

Yet while there was popular support in Japan for a policy of neutrality and unprecedented opposition to the extension of the Security Pact even in revised form, Soviet efforts to pressure Japan into neutralism by tying the return of Habomai and Shikotan to American withdrawal from Japan and by firing rockets almost directly over Japan in January 1960 aroused public resentment, for the Japanese people felt that the matter was an internal affair in which the USSR had no right to interfere.[7] Although the Soviet peace offensive continued and the USSR played on the fears of the Japanese public concerning atomic weapons and nuclear submarines,[8] the tone gradually softened by 1963, and Soviet protests were limited to radio broadcasts and newspaper articles rather than diplomatic notes.

Soviet charges that the extension of the Security Pact in June 1970 would prevent the development of economic relations between Japan and the USSR[9] did not

6. Tokuda Kyuichi "Nihon kyosanto no shin koryo no kiso" in *Nihon kyosanto tosei koyo bunken* (Tokyo, 1952), p. 51; "Soren no tainichi churitsuka seisaku," n. 31; see also Nozako Sanzo's speech in the plenary session of the House of Councillors on 27 June 1959 and in the Budget Committee of the House of Councillors on 5 March 1960, in Nihon kyosanto chuo iinkai, *Nozako Sanzo senshu sengo hen*, January 1946-February 1961 (Tokyo, 1966), pp. 344–47.

7. George R. Packard III, *Protest in Tokyo: The Security Treaty Crisis of 1960* (Princeton, 1966); *Asahi*, 29 January and 1 February 1960; *Sankei*, 29 January 1960; *Mainichi*, 29 January 1960; *Nihon Keizai*, 30 January 1960; and *Yomiuri*, 30 January 1960.

8. See Ikeda-Khrushchev correspondence in *Nihon Soren koryu nenshi*, 1961, and Moscow broadcasts reproduced in *Nisso kan juyo kokan bunsho*, no. 26, pp. 90, 99–101.

9. *Pravda*, 28 June 1970, 30 June 1970, 3 August 1970 in *Soren kankei juyo jiko nenshi*, 1970, pp. 180, 183.

hold true. Cordial relations had been established in many areas following normalization. Even in 1960, when strained political relations affected the fishery negotiations, great progress was registered in Soviet-Japanese trade.[10] Both governments learned to be realistic and not to allow their differences on one issue to affect all aspects of their relations.

The good relations helped to solve a number of minor problems. For example, in June 1963 an agreement was signed regarding the collection of sea tangle in the seas around Kaigarashima (near Habomai and Shikotan).[11] Permission was granted to Japanese to visit graves in the Soviet Union. Until 1959, only Japanese embassy personnel were allowed to visit Japanese graves in the neighbourhood of Moscow, Irkutsk, and Pavlovsk. In 1961, a delegation of thirty-three relatives of the deceased were permitted to visit Pavlovsk and Chita. Subsequently annual visits were allowed. In 1964 visits to graves in Habomai and Shikotan were permitted also, and in August 1969, to graves in Kunashiri.[12]

The facilities granted by the USSR to Japan Airlines to fly over Siberia *en route* to Europe were another expression of Soviet goodwill towards Japan, the Japanese line being the first foreign line to get such permission. In 1967, only joint operation was allowed, but in March 1970, independent DC-8 passenger flights of the Japan Airlines were authorized.[13]

The Soviet Union pushed for a cultural agreement with

10. *Nihon Keizai,* 3 March 1960.
11. *Nihon Soren koryu nenshi,* 1963, pp. 90–91.
12. *Nihon Soren koryu nenshi,* 1961, p. 167; 1964, p. 70; "Nisso kankei no keiei to genjo," *Chosa geppo,* June 1966, p. 12; *Japan Times,* 22 August 1969.
13. *Soren kankei juyo jiko nenshi,* 1967, p. 116; 1969, pp. 230–1; 1970, p. 174.

Japan. In 1962 the chairman of the Committee for Overseas Cultural Exchange, G. A. Zhukov, visited Japan for this purpose. Although no comprehensive agreement was signed because the Japanese government objected to the provisions that the expenses of a cultural delegation be borne fully by the host country and that the two governments assist and promote the cultural exchange even at the people's level,[14] short-term agreements about the exchange of scholars, scientists and experts and about the holding of film festivals followed. An exchange at the people's level ensued also, particularly in the wake of the Sino-Soviet rift, as the USSR competed with China in hosting groups of foreign visitors.

Leftist elements in Japan echoed the Soviet line of opposition to the United States and monopoly-capitalism and showed a genuine desire to strengthen the ties and friendship with socialist countries. This common outlook did not ensure, however, full support by all leftists of Soviet policies that affected Japanese national interests. Thus while the Japanese Communist Party adhered to the Soviet line on the territorial and fishery questions, the Japanese Socialist Party did not accept all Soviet claims, though its criticism of the socialist state was relatively soft because of the genuine belief that the USSR could be persuaded to modify her position, which, it was thought, was so hard due to the pro-American policies of the reactionary Japanese government. In the case of the suspension of nuclear tests, the Socialist and Communist Parties were embarrassed by the shift in Soviet policy, when the USSR on 30 August 1961 announced the resumption of nuclear tests. The Communist Party recovered from the embarrassment and defended the Soviet tests as "an appropriate measure to defend world peace", but the Social-

14. *Nihon Soren koryu nenshi,* 1962, p. 52.

ist Party vainly appealed to the USSR to reverse her decision, as the Japanese people opposed the tests.[15]

The Sino-Soviet rift led to a division of loyalties among Japanese leftists. While declaring that the problem posed for them by the Sino-Soviet dispute was not so simple as to choose which side to support, the Socialists criticized the USSR for "the tendency to claim her own national interests as the interests of the world proletariat" and for hurting movements in other countries by imposing her foreign policy on them. At the same time, they admitted the futility of mechanically applying an ideology, based on the historical and social conditions of another country, to the peace movement in Japan.[16]

The Japanese Communist Party long avoided taking a stand in the Sino-Soviet split, calling it a "figment of bourgeois imagination." When the split was brought into the open by Khrushchev through his attack on Albania in October 1961, the party adopted a tactic of neutralism, to which it clung through the crises over India, Yugoslavia and Cuba. But after the ninth conference of the Japan Council Against Atomic and Hydrogen Weapons (*Gensuikyo*) in August 1963, the Japanese Communist Party broke with the Communist Party of the USSR and attacked it bitterly. The Soviets responded by supporting the "Voice of Japan," a splinter group of the Japanese Communist Party, and by paying more attention to the Socialist Party.[17]

The split with Moscow put the Japanese Communist Party in the Chinese camp, but only temporarily. Imbued with a new sense of independence and autonomy, it dis-

15. Robert A. Scalapino, *The Japanese Communist Movement, 1920–1966* (Berkeley and Los Angeles, 1967), p. 120–25.

16. "What Should Our Attitude be Toward Moscow-Peking Conflict," *Japan Socialist Review,* 15 August 1963, pp. 15–19.

17. For a full discussion, see Scalapino, pp. 97 ff.

agreed with China's position on the abortive Communist coup in Indonesia in September 1965, which it regarded as "left-wing adventurism," and was unhappy about the refusal of the Chinese Communist Party to respond to its appeal for an international united front in support of the Vietnamese Communists. Resolutions passed at the Tenth Congress of the Japanese Communist Party in October 1966 attacked both Soviet "revisionism" and Chinese "dogmatism" and "sectarianism."[18] As the Japanese Communist Party, accusing Peking of seeking to push it into an armed struggle, broke with the Chinese Communist Party in 1967, Moscow was quick to normalize relations with it, for the "Voice of Japan" had failed to attract more than ten per cent of the Communists in Japan.[19]

In January 1968 a delegation led by M. A. Suslov, Secretary of the Central Committee of the Communist Party of the Soviet Union, conferred with the leadership of the Communist Party of Japan. They recognized the existence of ideological differences between them, but agreed to cooperate, respecting the principles of autonomy, equality and noninterference in each other's internal affairs. The Soviet side did not demand the reinstatement of the "Voice of Japan" into the regular Communist Party of Japan, admitting that this was an internal matter.[20] The principle of mutual noninterference in each other's affairs was reiterated by the Communist Parties of the USSR and Japan in a joint communiqué on 19 March 1971.[21]

18. "Principal Foreign Policies of the Four Parties in Japan," *The Japan Annual of International Affairs*, no. 3, 1963–1964, p. 186; J. A. A. Stockwin, "The Communist Party of Japan," *Problems of Communism*, vol. 16, January-February 1967, pp. 1–10.

19. Shigeo Omori, "Realignment of the JCP," *Japan Quarterly*, vol. 15, October-December 1967, pp. 443–50; Scalapino, pp. 303–5.

20. *Asian Almanac*, p. 3046.

21. *Konnichi no Sorenpo*, no. 8, 15 April 1971, p. 20.

The normalization of relations with the Japanese Communist Party revived Soviet political influence, as the membership of the Japanese Communist Party increased to 300,000 in 1971 and the circulation of the daily edition of its newspaper *Akahata* reached 420,000 and of the Sunday edition 1,470,000.[22] Deemphasizing ideological propaganda and advocating the parliamentary road to democracy, the Japanese Communist Party strove to recapture the image of a "lovable party," created in the early days of the Occupation.[23]

22. *Japan Times Weekly,* 2 January 1971; *Asahi* 13 April 1971; *Yomiuri* (evening) 29 June 1971.

23. Nozaka's appeal to the voters on the eve of the House of Councillors elections in June 1971, in Tokyo To Senkyo Kanri Iinkai, *Sangiin (Tokyo to senshutsu), giin senkyo kokoku,* 27 June 1971, page 3.

Epilogue

In the decades prior to the Pacific War the American desire to contain Russian expansion had facilitated Japanese acquisition of control over Korea and of a foothold in Manchuria. In the years after the Pacific War, American exclusion of the USSR from the Occupation had saved Japan from the agony of division, and the United States, which Japan had sought to drive out of East Asia, protected Japan's security and territorial integrity.

With the establishment of the Chinese People's Republic, the United States, though it had been drawn into the Pacific War by Japanese hostilities in China, blocked the normalization of Japanese relations with the mainland. Japan bowed to American pressure, conscious that her economic reconstruction and reentry into the comity of nations depended on the patronage of the United States. But the Soviet Union rallied to the support of the Chinese People's Republic and concluded with her a military alliance, directed specifically against Japan and Japan's allies. Thus, in spite of Japan's elimination from Korea, Manchuria and China proper, the USSR and Japan remained in rival camps.

In the past, the depiction of Russia as the traditional enemy in the north and ideological differences had not stood in the way of joint action against a third power whenever their mutual national interests required. In the decade before the Russian Revolution, the two countries came close to making the Far East their exclusive domain. When the Washington Conference restricted Japanese naval expansion, Japan veered toward the Soviet Union and in 1925 concluded a basic convention with her. From 1925 until 1937 the two powers cooperated in Manchuria,[1] and they remained on relatively good terms throughout most of the Pacific War. On the other hand, Japan had no qualms about soliciting a military alliance with the United States, by whom she was occupied, when the latter seemed the stronger of the two superpowers.

Japan did not fail to take advantage of the détente in East-West relations. Yet the protracted negotiations that led to the normalization of Japanese-Soviet relations showed that the nature and the timing of the decision on the Japanese side were the product of personal ambitions of party leaders in faction-ridden politics more than of national interest and were not guided by public opinion. Disunity within government circles on this issue weakened Japan's bargaining position. American attempts to influence the Japanese decision stiffened the attitude of the USSR, which used the fishery issue as a lever to hasten the normalization of relations without giving in on the territorial issue.

The restoration of diplomatic relations set the pace for the strengthening of economic ties, neither country allowing ideological differences to interfere with trade. The neighbouring Soviet Union was a convenient source for many of the raw materials needed by Japanese industry, while Japanese industry could play a vital part in the development of Siberia and the Russian Far East. The absence of a peace treaty, even the extension of the Japanese-American Security Pact and the lingering dis-

1. See G. A. Lensen, *The Damned Inheritance: The Soviet Union and the Manchurian Crises, 1924–1935.*

pute about the territorial question, did not impair the steady development of Japanese-Soviet economic ties.

The Sino-Soviet split increased the importance of good relations with Japan for the USSR. The humiliating disregard of Japanese interests and pride inherent in the unexpected American restrictions on imports in 1971 and President Richard M. Nixon's dramatic visit to Peking the following year made collaboration with the USSR increasingly attractive for Japan. Premier Tanaka Kakuei outdid President Nixon by establishing diplomatic relations with the Chinese People's Republic, but this did not lessen Soviet efforts to improve relations with Japan; if anything, it gave them greater urgency. On the other hand, with the apparent Soviet-American rapprochement and the growth of Soviet-American trade, a new source of funds and aid became available to the USSR. The introduction of this competitive element stood to make the Japanese less reluctant to finance economic ventures in the USSR and made possible a new era of development in Siberia through combined Soviet-American-Japanese efforts.

Documents

A

Convention Concerning The High Seas Fisheries of the Northwest Pacific Ocean [1]

(Unofficial Translation)

The Governments of Japan and the Union of Soviet Socialist Republics,

Considering the common interest of the Contracting Parties with respect to the development, on a rational basis, of the fisheries in the Northwest Pacific Ocean, and their mutual responsibility with respect to the condition of the fish and other marine living resources, as well as to the effective utilization of those resources,

Recognizing that it will serve the common interest of mankind, as well as the interests of the Contracting Parties to maintain the maximum sustained productivity of fisheries in the Northwest Pacific Ocean,

Considering that each of the Contracting Parties should assume an obligation, on a free and equal footing, to conserve and increase the above mentioned resources,

1. *The Japanese Annual of International Law 1957.*

Recognizing that it is highly desirable to promote and coordinate the scientific studies of the Contracting Parties, the purpose of which is to maintain the maximum sustained productivity of fisheries of interest to the two Contracting Parties,

Have therefore, decided to conclude this Convention, and for this purpose have appointed their respective representatives who have agreed as follows:

ARTICLE I

1. The area to which this Convention applies, hereinafter referred to as "the Convention area," shall be all waters, other than territorial waters, of the Northwest Pacific Ocean, including the Japan Sea, the Okhotsk Sea and the Bering Sea.

2. Nothing in this Convention shall be deemed to affect in any way the position of the Contracting Parties in regard to the limits of territorial sea or to the jurisdiction over fisheries.

ARTICLE II

1. The Contracting Parties in order to conserve and develop the fish and other marine living resources, hereinafter referred to as the "fishery resources," agree to carry out in the Convention area, the co-ordinated measures specified in the Annex to this Convention.

2. The Annex attached hereto shall form an integral part of this Convention. All references to the "Convention" shall be understood as including the said Annex either in its present terms or as revised in accordance with the provisions of paragraph (a) of Article IV.

ARTICLE III

1. In order to realize the objectives of this Convention, the Contracting Parties shall establish the Japan-Soviet Northwest Pacific Fisheries Commission, hereinafter referred to as "the Commission."

2. The Commission shall be composed of two national

sections, each consisting of three members appointed by the governments of the respective Contracting Parties.

3. All resolutions, recommendations and other decisions oi the Commission shall be made only by agreement between ih͜ national sections.

4. The Commission may decide upon and revise, as occasion may require, the rules for the conduct of its meetings.

5. The Commission shall meet at least once each year and at such other times as may be requested by one of the national sections. The date and place of the first meeting shall be determined by agreement between the Contracting Parties.

6. At its first meeting the Commission shall select a Chairman and Vice-Chairman from different national sections. The Chairman and Vice-Chairman shall hold office for a period of one year. The selection of a Chairman and Vice-Chairman from the national sections shall be made in such a manner as will yearly provide each Contracting Party in turn with representation in those offices.

7. The official languages of the Commission shall be Japanese and Russian.

8. The expenses incurred by a member of the Commission in connection with participation in the meetings of the Commission shall be paid by the appointing government. Joint expenses incurred by the Commission shall be paid by the Commission through contributions made by the Contracting Parties in the form and proportion recommended by the Commission and approved by the Contracting Parties.

ARTICLE IV

The Commission shall perform the following functions:

(a) At the regular annual meeting, consider the appropriateness of co-ordinated measure being enforced at the time, and if necessary revise the Annex to this Convention. Such revision shall be determined on the basis of scientific findings.

(b) When it is required by the Annex to fix the total annual catch of a stock of fish, determine the total annual catch of such stock by the Contracting Parties and notify the said Parties.

(c) Determine the kind and scope of statistics and other reports to be submitted to the Commission by each of the Contracting Parties for carrying out the provisions of this Convention.

(d) For the purpose of studying the fishery resources, prepare and adjust co-ordinated scientific research programs and recommend them to the Contracting Parties.

(e) Submit annually to the Contracting Parties a report on the operations of the Commission.

(f) In addition to the functions stipulated above, make recommendations to the Contracting Parties with respect to the matter of conservation and increase of fishery resources in the Convention area.

ARTICLE V

The Contracting Parties agree, for the purpose of mutually exchanging experiences concerning the study and conservation of fishery resources and the regulation of fisheries, to exchange men of learning and experience in fisheries. The exchange of such men shall be conducted by agreement from time to time between the two Parties.

ARTICLE VI

1. The Contracting Parties shall take appropriate and effective measures in order to carry out the provisions of this Convention.

2. When in receipt of the notification from the Commission concerning the total annual catch fixed for each of the Contracting Parties in accordance with paragraph (b) of Article IV, the Contracting Parties shall issue a license or a certificate to their fishing vessels and inform each other of all such licenses and certificates issued.

3. The licenses and certificates issued by the Contracting Parties shall be in both the Japanese and Russian Languages, and the fishing vessels, when engaged in fishing operations,

shall have on board their license or certificate without fail.

4. The Contracting Parties agree, for the purpose of rendering effective the provisions of this Convention, to enact and enforce necessary laws and regulations, with regard to their nationals, organizations and fishing vessels, with appropriate penalties against violations thereof and to submit to the Commission a report on any action taken by them with regard thereto.

ARTICLE VII

1. When authorized officials of either of the Contracting Parties have reasonable ground to believe that a fishing vessel of other Party is actually violating the provisions of this Convention, such officials may board and search the vessel to ascertain whether the said provisions are being observed.

Such officials shall present credentials issued by their Government and written in both the Japanese and Russian languages, if requested by the master of the vessel.

2. If it becomes clear as a result of the search conducted by such officials that there is evidence that the fishing vessel or any person on board such vessel is violating the Convention, the said officials may seize such vessel or arrest such person.

In that case, the Contracting Party to which the officials belong shall notify as soon as possible the other Contracting Party to which such fishing vessel or person belongs of the arrest or seizure, and shall deliver such vessel or person as promptly as practicable to the authorized officials of the Contracting Party to which the vessel or person belongs at the place of arrest or seizure unless another place is agreed upon by the Contracting Parties. Provided, however, that when the Contracting Party which receives such notification cannot immediately accept delivery and requests of the other Contracting Party, the latter Party receiving the request may keep such vessel or person under surveillance within its own territory, under the conditions agreed upon by the Contracting Parties.

3. Only the authorities of the Party to which the above mentioned fishing vessel or person belongs have jurisdiction to try cases arising in connection with this Article and impose penalties therefor. Written evidence and proof establishing the offense shall be furnished as promptly as possible to the Contracting Party having jurisdiction to try the case.

ARTICLE VIII

1. This Convention shall become effective from the date of entry into force of the Peace Treaty between Japan and the Union of Soviet Socialist Republics or from the date of the restoration of diplomatic relations between the said countries.

2. After this Convention has remained in force for a period of ten years, either Contracting Party may give notice to the other Contracting Party of the intention to abrogate the said Convention, and it shall terminate one year after the date of receipt of the said notification by the latter Party.

In Witness Whereof, the undersigned representatives have signed this Treaty.

Done in duplicate, in the Japanese and Russian languages, both equally authentic, at Moscow, this fourteenth day of May, one thousand nine hundred and fifty-six.

By Authority of the Government of Japan:

ad referendum

I. Kono

K. Matsudaira

By Authority of the Government of the Union of Soviet Socialist Republics:

A. Ishkov

Annex

The Contracting Parties agree to regulate, within the Convention area, the fishing of the stocks of fish named below:

1. Salmon

Chum Salmon (Oncorhynchus keta)

Pink Salmon (Oncorhynchus gorbuscha)

Silver Salmon (Oncorhynchus kisutch)
Sokeye Salmon (Oncorhynchus nerka)
King Salmon (Oncorhynchus tschawytscha)

(a) The area wherein the fishing will be regulated shall be the Northwest Pacific Ocean (including the Okhotsk Sea and Bering Sea) bounded on the east and south by a line running southeast from Cape Navarin to the intersection of 55° North latitude and 175° West longitude; thence south to the intersection of 45° North latitude and 175° West longitude; thence west to the intersection of 45° North latitude and 155° East longitude; thence southwest to Akiyuri Island; and the Japan Sea north of 45° North latitude.

(b) With regard to the fishing season for 1956, sea-fishery with movable fishing gear shall be prohibited in the Convention area within forty nautical miles from the coastline of the islands belonging to either of the Contracting Parties and from the continental coast within the area stipulated (a). Based upon scientific data, such prohibited areas shall be re-examined by the Commission as soon as practicable.

These regulations prohibiting sea-fishery with movable fishing gear shall not apply to small Japanese fishing vessels in the waters adjacent to Hokkaido within the prohibited area.

(c) The total amount of catch shall be determined by the Commission. The total amount of catch for the first year the Convention is in effect shall be determined at the first meeting of the Commission.

(d) With respect to mothership-type fishing operations, the catch per year (in raw fish weight) by each fishing vessel and investigation ship shall not exceed three hundred metric tons and one hundred and fifty metric tons respectively.

The total amount of catch by all the fishing vessels and investigation ships belonging to a mothership shall not exceed the total catch fixed for such mothership. Within the scope of such total catch the catch by each fishing vessel and investigation vessel may exceed to some degree the above amounts fixed for each fishing vessel and investigation vessel respectively.

(e) The fishing season for each year shall end on 10 August.

(f) The length of drifting nets set in the sea by a fishing vessel shall be as follows:

Not more than ten kilometres in the Okhotsk Sea; not more than twelve kilometres in the waters of the Pacific Ocean bounded on the east and south by the line connecting Cape Olyutorskiy, the intersection of 48° North latitude and 170° 25′ East longitude, and Akiyuri Island; not more than fifteen kilometres in the other areas.

The distance between the drifting nets set by a fishing vessel shall be that confirmed immediately after the setting, and the distance between one net and the nearest net shall, in any direction, be as follows:

Not less than twelve kilometres in the Okhotsk Sea area; not less than ten kilometres in the waters of the Pacific Ocean bounded on the east and south by the line connecting Cape Olyutorskiy, the intersection of 48° North latitude and 170° 25′ East longitude, and Akiyuri Island; not less than eight kilometres in the other areas.

These provisions, however, shall not apply to small fishing vessels operating in the waters south of 48° North latitude and having their base of operations at a port in Japan.

With respect to meshes of drifting net, the length from knot to knot shall be not less than fifty-five millimetres.

2. Herring (Clupea Pallasii)

Fishing of small immature herring of less than twenty centimetres in length (from tip of snout to the end of vertebral column at the caudal fin) shall be prohibited.

Incidental catch of such small herrings, if not in large quantity, shall be allowed. The allowable extent of such catch shall be determined by the Commission.

3. Crabs

King Crabs (Paralithodes camtschatica)
　　　　　　(Paralithodes platypus)

(a) Fishing of female crab and immature crab whose carapace is less than thirteen centimetres in width shall be prohibited. The female crabs and the afore-mentioned immature crabs if caught in the nets shall be released back into the water immediately.

The incidental catch of female crabs and above-mentioned immature crabs, if not in large quantity shall be allowed. The allowable extent of such catch shall be determined by the Commission.

The Commission shall also determine the amount of incidental catch of female and above-mentioned immature crabs in a given area requiring suspension of fishing in that area.

(b) In consideration of conservation of the resources, as well as efficiency of operations, restrictions shall be placed upon the length of the row of crab nets, the distance between the nets arranged in a row, and the distance separating the several rows. The commission shall determine the restrictions.

B

Agreement For Cooperation
For The Rescue of Persons
In Distress at Sea[2]

(Unofficial Translation)

The Governments of Japan and the Union of Soviet Socialist Republics,

Recognizing the need for making an arrangement to render
possible cooperation for giving prompt and effective assistance,
irrespective of nationality, to persons in distress in the Japan
Sea, the Okhotsk Sea, the Bering Sea, and in the waters of
the Northwest Pacific Ocean adjacent to the coasts of Japan
and the Union of Soviet Socialist Republics,

Have for this purpose appointed their respective representatives who have agreed as follows:

ARTICLE I

1. In case any vessel (the term "vessel" as used in this
Agreement is understood to include fishing vessels) is in
distress in the Japan Sea, the Okhotsk Sea, the Bering Sea or
in the waters of the Northwest Pacific Ocean adjacent to the

2. *Ibid.*

158

coasts of Japan and the Union of Soviet Socialist Republics (hereinafter referred to as "the Soviet Union"), the sea disaster rescue agencies of the Contracting Parties shall give necessary assistance, to the furthest extent possible, in rescuing persons on board such vessel.

2. When a sea disaster rescue agency of either Contracting Party receives a report of a vessel in distress at sea, the agency concerned shall take the rescue measures deemed most appropriate with respect to persons on board such vessel.

3. In case the place of disaster is located near the coast of the other Contracting Party, or when it is deemed necessary, the sea disaster rescue agency receiving the information of the disaster shall make plans for rescue operations after consultation with the sea disaster rescue agency of the other Contracting Party.

Such consultation shall be held invariably when the sea disaster rescue agency of one Contracting Party receives a report that a vessel belonging to the other Contracting Party is in distress at sea.

ARTICLE II

The rescue operations within the territorial sea of Japan or of the Soviet Union shall be conducted in accordance with the laws and regulations of the country concerned.

ARTICLE III

1. The wireless stations of the sea disaster rescue agencies of Japan and the Soviet Union shall receive the distress signals sent in frequencies of 500 kilocycles (600 metres) and 2,182 kilocycles (137.5 metres) in compliance with the international regulations concerning transmission and receipt of distress signals.

2. Wireless contact between the sea disaster rescue agencies of Japan and the Soviet Union shall be made through Station JNL with respect to the rescue agency of Japan and Station URH with respect to the rescue agency of the Soviet Union.

In this event, call signals shall be made in the frequency of 500 kilocycles, and subsequent transmission in the case of Station JNL shall be in frequencies of 472 kilocycles, or 3,212.5 kilocycles at night and 6,386.5 kilocycles during the day, and in the case of Station URH in frequencies of 457 kilocycles, or 3,270 kilocycles at night and 6,365 kilocycles during the day. When call signals are made in the frequency of 500 kilocycles and if reliable wireless contact cannot be made at a certain time of the day or night, sea disaster rescue agencies of the Contracting Parties may agree to make the call signals at such times in the other frequencies stipulated in this Convention.

3. The ships belonging to the sea disaster rescue agencies while conducting rescue operations shall maintain wireless contact with each other, as well as with the vessel in distress through Station JNL and Station URH respectively, and if necessary may make direct contact in frequencies of 500 kilocycles or 2,182 kilocycles.

4. The wireless communications mentioned in 1, 2, and 3 above shall be made in international code or when possible in the ordinary English language.

ARTICLE IV

1. The sea disaster rescue agency of either Contracting Party that commences rescue operations first for the purpose of rendering assistance may when necessary for completion of the operations request the cooperation of the rescue agency of the other Contracting Party, in accordance with the provisions of Article III.

2. The sea disaster rescue agency in receipt of the request mentioned above shall as far as practicable despatch means of rescue to the reported place of disaster for the purpose of rescue operations.

ARTICLE V

The Contracting Parties undertake to give detailed instructions concerning enforcement of the provisions of this Agreement to their respective sea disaster rescue agencies.

ARTICLE VI

The provisions of this agreement shall not be deemed to be in conflict with the Convention for the unification of certain rules respecting assistance and salvage at sea signed at Brussels on 23 September 1910 and the International Convention for the Safety of Life at Sea, 1948, signed at London on 10 June 1948.

ARTICLE VII

1. This Agreement shall become effective from the date of entry into force of the Peace Treaty between Japan and the Union of Soviet Socialist Republics or from the date of restoration of diplomatic relations between the said countries, and remain in force for a period of three years.

2. If neither of the Contracting Parties announces the abrogation of this Agreement at least one year before the above mentioned period expires, it shall continue in force for another three years, and it shall continue to remain in force for additional periods of three years each as long as neither of the Contracting Parties announces the abrogation of this Agreement as least one year before the expiration of each extended period of three years.

In Witness Whereof, the undersigned representatives have signed this convention.

Done in duplicate, in the Japanese and Russian languages, both equally authentic, at Moscow, this fourteeth day of May, one thousand nine hundred fifty-six.

By authority of the Government of Japan
ad referendum

I. Kono
K. Matsudaira

By authority of the Government of the Union of Soviet Socialist Republics

A. Ishkov

C

Joint Declaration[3]

(Unofficial Translation)

Negotiations were conducted in Moscow from October 13 to October 19, 1956, between the Delegations of Japan and of the Union of Soviet Socialist Republics.

From the Japanese side there participated
Ichiro Hatoyama, Prime Minister,
Ichiro Kono, Minister of Agriculture and Forestry,
Shunichi Matsumoto, Member of the House of Representatives.

From the side of the Union of Soviet Socialist Republics there participated
N. A. Bulganin, Chairman of the Council of Ministers of the Soviet Union,
N. S. Khruchchev, Member of the Presidium of the Supreme Soviet of the Soviet Union,
A. I. Mikoyan, First Deputy Chairman of the Council of Ministers of the Soviet Union,
A. A. Gromyko, First Deputy Minister for Foreign Affairs of the Soviet Union,
N. T. Fedorenko, Deputy Minister for Foreign Affairs of the Soviet Union.

Through the negotiations conducted in an atmosphere of

3. *Ibid.*

162

mutual understanding and cooperation, a frank and extensive exchange of views was made on the mutual relations between Japan and the Union of Soviet Socialist Republics. Japan and the Union of Soviet Socialist Republics fully agreed that the reestablishment of diplomatic relations between the two countries would contribute to the promotion of understanding and cooperation between them in the interests of peace and security in the Far East.

As a result of these negotiations conducted between the Delegations of Japan and of the Union of Soviet Socialist Republics, the following was agreed upon:

1. The state of war between Japan and the Union of Soviet Socialist Republics is terminated as from the date on which the present Declaration enters into force, and relations of peace ,amity and good neighourhood shall be restored between them.

2. Diplomatic and consular relations shall be reestablished between Japan and the Union of Soviet Socialist Republics. The two countries shall exchange without delay diplomatic envoys of ambassadorial rank. The matters relating to the establishment of the respective consular offices in each other's country shall be dealt with through the diplomatic agencies.

3. Japan and the Union of Soviet Socialist Republics confirm that they will be guided in their mutual relations by the principles of the Charter of the United Nations and in particular the following principles set forth in Article 2 thereof:

(a) to settle their international disputes by peaceful means in such a manner that international peace and security, and justice are not endangered;

(b) to refrain in their international relations from the threat or use of force against the territorial integrity or political independence of any State or in any other manner inconsistent with the Purposes of the United Nations.

Japan and the Union of Soviet Socialist Republics confirm that each other country possesses the inherent right of individual or collective self-defense referred to in Article 51 of the Charter of the United Nations.

Japan and the Union of Soviet Socialist Republics mutually undertake that they will not intervene, either directly or indirectly, in the internal affairs of each other, regardless of whether for economic, political or ideological reasons.

4. The Union of Soviet Socialist Republics shall support the application by Japan for membership in the United Nations.

5. All Japanese nationals convicted in the Union of Soviet Socialist Republics shall be released upon the entry into force of the present Joint Declaration and be repatriated to Japan.

The Union of Soviet Socialist Republics shall, in compliance with the request of Japan, continue investigations on missing Japanese nationals.

6. The Union of Soviet Socialist Republics waives all reparations claims against Japan.

Japan and the Union of Soviet Socialist Republics mutually waive all claims of the respective State and its organizations and nationals against the other State and its organizations and nationals arising out of the war since August 9, 1945.

7. Japan and the Union of Soviet Socialist Republics agree to enter into negotiations as soon as possible for the conclusion of treaties or agreements to place their trading, maritime and other commercial relations on a stable and friendly basis.

8. The Convention between Japan and the Union of Soviet Socialist Republics concerning the Fisheries in the High Seas of the Northwest Pacific Ocean and the Agreement between Japan and the Union of Soviet Socialist Republics concerning cooperation for the Rescue of Persons in Distress at Sea, which were signed in Moscow on May 14, 1956, shall become effective simultaneously with the entry into force of the present Declaration.

Japan and the Union of Soviet Socialist Republics shall in a spirit of cooperation take measures for the conservation and development of fishery resources as well as for the regulation and restriction of fishing in the high seas, taking into consideration the interests of Japan and the Union of Soviet Socialist Republics with regard to the conservation and rational utilization of the fish and other living resources of the sea.

9. Japan and the Union of Soviet Socialist Republics agree to continue their negotiations for the conclusion of a peace treaty after normal diplomatic relations have been reestablished between the two countries.

The Union of Soviet Socialist Republics, in response to the desire of Japan and in consideration of her interests, agrees to transfer the Habomai Islands and the island of Shikotan to Japan, provided, however, that the actual transfer of these islands shall be effected after the peace treaty between Japan and the Union of Soviet Socialist Republics is concluded.

10. The present Joint Declaration shall be ratified. It shall enter into force on the date of exchange of instruments of ratification. The instruments of ratification shall be exchanged in Tokyo as soon as possible.

In Witness Whereof, the undersigned Plenipotentiaries have signed the present Joint Declaration.

Done in duplicate, in the Japanese and Russian languages, both equally authentic, in Moscow, this nineteenth day of October, 1956.

By authority of the Government of Japan

> Ichiro Hatoyama
> Ichiro Kono
> Shunichi Matsumoto

By authority of the Presidium of the Supreme Soviet of the Union of Soviet Socialist Republics

> N. Bulganin
> D. Shepilov

D

Protocol Concerning the Development of Trade and the Mutual Granting of Most-Favoured-Nation Treatment[4]

(Unofficial Translation)

In connection with the provisions of item 7 of the Joint Declaration by Japan and the Union of Soviet Socialist Republics, signed in Moscow on October 19, 1956, the Government of Japan and the Government of the Union of Soviet Socialist Republics have agreed as follows:

1. Pending the conclusion of the treaties or agreements envisaged in item 7 of the above-mentioned Joint Declaration, both Contracting Parties will endeavour as much as possible to develop trade between the two countries, and, for this purpose, each Contracting Party shall accord to the other the following treatment:

(a) most-favoured-nation treatment with respect to cus-

4. *Ibid.*

toms duties and charges of any kind as well as customs formalities and other regulations, on the importation to its territory of products of the other Party and the exportation of its products to the territory of such other Party;

(b) most-favoured-nation treatment with respect to vessel of the other Party at ports and harbours, inter alia their entry to, departure from and stay in the ports and harbours, charges and fees of any kind, loading and unloading of cargoes, and supply of fuel, water and food.

2. Nothing in the preceding paragraph shall limit the the right of either Contracting Party to enforce prohibitions or restrictions of any kind directed to the protection of its essential security interests.

The present Protocol shall be ratified. It shall enter into force on the date of exchange of instruments of ratification. The instruments of ratification shall be exchanged in Tokyo as soon as possible.

In Witness Whereof, the undersigned Plenipotentiaries have signed the present Protocol.

Done in duplicate, in the Japanese and Russian languages, both equally authentic, in Moscow, this nineteenth day of October, 1956.

By authority of the Government of Japan
                    Ichiro Hatoyama
                    Ichiro Kono
                    Shunichi Matsumoto

By authority of the Presidium of the Supreme Soviet of the Union of Soviet Socialist Republics
                    N. Bulganin
                    D. Shepilov

E

Japanese Trade With The USSR[5]

Year	Total exports	Total imports	(in thousand dollars) Balance
1958	18,103	22,164	−4,061
1959	23,027	39,485	−16,458
1960	59,976	87,020	−27,044
1961	65,380	145,019	−79,639
1962	149,390	147,276	+2,104
1963	158,136	161,940	−3,804
1964	181,811	226,729	−44,918
1965	168,358	240,198	−71,840
1966	214,024	300,361	−86,337
1967	157,688	453,918	−296,230
1968	179,018	463,512	−284,504
1969	268,247	461,563	−193,316
1970	340,932	481,038	−140,096

5. Japan, Ministry of International Trade and Industry, *Sengo Nihon no boeki nijunen shi* (Tokyo, 1967), pp. 442–43; *Tsusho hakusho* 1969 (Kakuron), pp. 625–27; 1971, (Kakuron), pp. 708–710.

Japan's Major Exports to USSR [6]

(in thousand dollars)

Product	1958	1959	1960	1961	1962	1963
Textile products (including fibres)	5,203	4,846	9,167	12,219	23,973	23,696
Chemical products	678	679	1,333	718	2,565	4,638
Metal products	8,773	6,295	26,921	16,024	34,901	44,946
Machinery (of which ships)	2,364 (321)	9,223 (8,087)	18,195 (11,201)	27,180 (3,910)	81,603 (37,784)	76,872 (33,981)
Other light maufactured products	1,085	1,984	4,360	9,239	6,348	7,984

6. *Sengo no boeki nijunen shi*, pp. 442–43; *Tsusho hakusho* 1969 (Kakuron), pp. 625–26; 1971 (Kakuron), pp. 708–709.

Japan's Major Exports to USSR (Contd.)

(in thousand dollars)

Product	1964	1965	1966	1967	1968	1969	1970
Textile products (including fibres)	22,097	26,563	48,020	48,464	58,236	85,360	103,807
Chemical products	11,520	23,596	24,052	21,255	20,730	36,706	40,822
Metal products	16,636	36,649	34,435	21,513	30,775	45,136	55,188
Machinery (of which	117,026	63,067	92,466	53,055	50,301	73,969	108,717
ships)	(62,636)	(34,008)	(50,853)	(91)	(371)	(2,446)	(4,461)
Other light manufactured products	14,532	18,483	8,402	9,963	13,059	12,673	13,701

Japan's Major Imports from USSR [7]

(in thousand dollars)

Products	1958	1959	1960	1961	1962	1963
Food (fish and wheat)	1,110	2,791	6,484	4,539	4,302	3,837
Raw materials (raw cotton, chrome ore, scrap iron, lumber, asbestos)	8,558	18,248	26,186	32,539	44,716	41,102
of which						
raw cotton	(108)	(2,672)	(6,597)	(4,605)	(944)	(768)
Lumber	(7,910)	(12,362)	(15,605)	(23,633)	(37,768)	(33,946)
Mineral fuels	5,895	7,651	27,288	60,051	64,779	64,654
Coal	(5,717)	(5,046)	(7,680)	(13,253)	(17,040)	(14,885)
Oil and oil products	(178)	(2,275)	(18,846)	(46,454)	(47,372)	(49,504)
Chemical products	1,008	5,280	7,568	11,357	8,296	10,708
Machinery	—	—	—	—	—	—
Other products (pig iron, white metals, palladium, aluminum)	5,515	5,432	19,494	36,533	25,183	41,639

7. *Sengo no boeki nijunen shi*, pp. 442–43; *Tsusho hakusho* 1969 (Kakuron), pp. 627–28; 1971 (Kakuron), pp. 710–11.

Japan's Major Imports from USSR (Contd.)

(in thousand dollars)

Products	1964	1965	1966	1967	1968	1969	1970
Food (fish and wheat)	2,800	4,840	6,401	7,989	6,542	8,305	10,187
Raw materials (raw cotton, chrome ore, scrap iron, lumber asbestos) of which	68,742	81,514	116,976	204,743	260,410	264,189	272,166
cotton	(1,876)	(7,109)	(13,024)	(36,715)	(49,804)	(45,832)	(24,317)
Lumber	(50,576)	(58,308)	(76,463)	(119,533)	(164,038)	(170,199)	(197,712)
Mineral Fuels	74,623	78,330	90,512	96,374	81,950	67,422	76,194
Coal	(16,484)	(17,855)	(22,922)	(34,120)	(39,569)	(46,176)	(43,671)
Oil and oil products	(58,028)	(57,269)	(67,591)	(62,254)	(42,380)	(21,246)	(32,523)
Chemical products	7,820	8,819	8,931	12,020	10,857	9,605	12,015
Machinery	—	—	2,015	3,068	3,153	3,992	5,536
Other products (pig iron, white metals, palladium, aluminum)	72,744	66,695	75,457	129,624	100,420	107,648	103,024

Bibliography

WORKS IN JAPANESE
(All Japanese Language Publications are published in Tokyo)

Primary Sources

Hatoyama Ichiro. *Kaikoroku* (Memoirs), 1957.

Japan, Cabinet Research Office. *Sovieto nenpo* (Annual report of Soviet affairs), 1955, 1958, 1959.

————. *Soren kankei juyo jiko nenshi* (Annual record of important matters relating to the Soviet Union). 1965–1970.

————. *Chosa geppo* (Monthly review). 1955–1970.

Japan, House of Representatives, 25th Session, *Nisso kyodo sengen nado tokubetsu iinkai gijiroku* (Proceedings of the Special Committee on Joint Declaration with the Soviet Union). 19–26 November 1956.

Japan, Ministry of Finance. *Nihon gaikoku boeki nenpyo* (*Kunibetsu*) (*Hinbetsu*), (Chronology of Japan's foreign trade) (countrywise) (commoditywise). 1947–1963.

Japan, Ministry of Foreign Affairs. *Shusen shiroku* (Historical record of the ending of the War). 1952

————. *Nihon gaiko nenpyo narabini shuyo bunsho* (Chronology and documents relating to Japan's foreign relations) *1840–1945*. 2 vols. 1955.

————. *Chukyo Tai-Nichi juyo genron* (Important speeches relating to Japan made by Communist China), *March 1956*. 1956.

————. *Waga gaiko no kinkyo* (The present state of our foreign relations). 1958– (Semi-annual publication).

————. *Hoppo ryodo* (Northern territories). 1961.

————. Ministry of International Trade and Industry. *Nisso*

boeki no genjo to mondaiten (The present state and problems in Japan-Soviet trade). 1958.

———. *Sengo Nihon no boeki nijunen shi: Nihon no hatten to henbo* (The twenty year history of postwar Japan's trade: Development and transfiguration of Japan). 1967.

———. *Tsusho hakusho* (*Soron*) (*Kakuron*) (White Paper on trade, General discussion as well as details regarding particular countries). 1968–1971.

Japan, National Diet Library. *Nisso kokko chosei mondai kiso shiryo shu* (Collection of basic material on the problem of the rectification of Japanese-Soviet diplomatic relations). 1955.

———. Newspapers Clipping Section, "Nisso kosho" (Japanese-Soviet negotiations), "Nisso gyogyo kosho" (Japanese-Soviet fishery negotiations), etc.

Kato Kanju. *Senryoka ni okeru soshireibu to no sessho* (Negotiations with the General Headquarters during the Occupation). n.d.

Kenpo Chosa Kai. *Kenpo chosa kai dai 3 iinkai dai 30 kai gijiroku* (Proceedings of the thirtieth meeting of the third sub-committee of the Constitution Research Council).

Kido Nikki Kenkyukai (ed.). *Kido koichi kankei bunsho* (Documents relating to Kido Koichi). 1966.

Kono Ichiro. *Ima dakara hanaso* (I may talk now). 1958.

Matsumoto Shunichi. *Moscow ni kakeru niji* (A rainbow bridge to Moscow). 1966.

Minshushugi Kenkyukai (ed.). *Nihon Soren koryu nenshi* (Annual record of Japanese-Soviet Exchanges). 1960, 1961, 1962, 1963, 1964.

Misuzu Shobo. *Gendai shi shiryo* (Materials relating to contemporary history) 10 *Nitchu senso* (Sino-Japanese War) (3), 1966.

Nanpo Doho Engokai. *Hoppo ryodo mondai kiso shiryo* (Basic materials relating to the Northern Territories). 1958.

Nihon Hyoron Sha. *Shiryo sengo nijunen shi* (Materials relating to twenty years of postwar history), *Seiji* (Politics), 1966.

————. *Shiryo sengo nijunen shi* (Materials relating to twenty years of postwar history), *Rodo* (Labour), 1966.

Nihon kyosanto chuo iinkai. *Senryoka Nihon no bunseki* (Analysis of Japan under Occupation). 2 vols. 1954.

Nihon kyosanto chuo iinkai. *Nosaka Sanzo senshu sengo hen* (Selections of Nozaka Sanzo's postwar speeches) *January 1946-February 1961.* 1966.

Nihon Shakaito. *Heiwa e no yuko: Shakaito ho So to-O shisetsudan hokoku* (Friendly approaches towards peace: Report of Japanese Socialist Party Delegation to the Soviet Union and East Europe). 1964.

Nihon Shakaito Hoppo Ryodo Mondai Tokubetsu Iinkai. *Hoppo ryodo mondai ni taisuru kenkai* (Views about the Northern Territorial Problem). Mimeographed, 1971.

Nikkan Rodo Tsushin Sha. *Sengo Nihon kyosanto bunken shu* (Collection of documents relating to postwar Japan Communist Party), vol. 4. 1953.

————. *Nisso kan juyo kokan bunsho* (Important documents exchanged between Japan and the USSR). 1964.

Nisso Shinzen Kyokai (ed.). *Soren wa Nihon ni nani wo nozomu ka* (What does the Soviet Union expect in Japan). 1949.

Nitchu Boeki Sokushin Giin Renmei (ed.). *Nitchu kankei shiryo shu* (Materials relating to Sino-Japanese Relations). 1967.

"Selected Archives of the Japanese Army, Navy and other Government Agencies 1868–1945," Microfilm Reproductions, T 1490 and T 1492 of Reel No. 220.

Secondary Sources

Fujiwara Hirotatsu. *Gendai Nihon no seiji ishiki,* (Political Consciousness in Modern Japan). 1958.

Hayashi Shigeru, et al. *Nihon shusen shi* (History of the end of the war in Japan). 1962.

Hirano Yoshitaro. *Gendai Chugoku to Chuso kankei* (Modern China and Sino-Soviet Relations). vol. 2. 1965.

Hosoya Chihiro. *Shiberia shuppei no shiteki kenkyu* (Historical Research of the Siberia Expedition). 1955.

Ishida Takeshi. *Hakyoku to heiwa* (Catastrophe and peace). 1968.

Kutakov, Leonid Nikolaevich. *Nisso gaiko kankei shi,* translated by Sovieto gaiko kenkyukai. 3 vols. 1965–1969.

Maruyama Masao. *Gendai seiji shiso to kodo* (Thought and behaviour in modern Japanese politics). 1968.

———. *Nihon no shiso* (Japanese thought). 1968.

Nihon Gaiko Gakkai (ed.). *Taiheiyo senso shuketsu ron* (End of the Pacific War). 1958.

Nihon Kokusai Mondai Kenkyujo. *Nihon no anzen hosho* (Security of Japan). 1967.

Nihon Kokusai Seiji Gakkai. Nihon gaiko no bunseki (Analysis of Japan's Foreign Relations). 1957.

———. *Gendai kokusai seiji no kozo* (Structure of international politics in modern times). 1958.

———. *Gendai kokusai seiji shi* (History of international politics in modern times). 1959.

———. *Futatsu no sekai to nashonarizumu* (Nationalism and the two worlds). 1959.

———. *Taiheiyo senso e no michi* (Road to the Pacific War) 7 vols. 1962–65.

———. *Nichiro Nisso kankei no tenkai* (Development of Russo-Japanese and Japan-Soviet Relations). 1966.

———. *Taigai seisaku no kettei katei* (Foreign policy decision-making process). 1959.

Nikkan Rodo Tsushin Sha. *Saikin ni okeru Nihon kyosanto no kihonteki senryaku to senjitsu* (Basic strategy and tactics of Japan Communist Party in recent times). 1953–1958.

———. *Rodo kumiai wo nerau Nihon kyosanto* (Japan Communist Party which aims at the Labour Unions). 1954.

———. *Sengo Nihon kyosanshugi undo* (The Communist movement in postwar Japan). 1955.

Nishimura Kumao. *Anzen hosho joyaku ron* (The Security Treaty). 1959.

Nisso Kyokai. *Nisso shinzen no shiori* (A guide to the friendship between Japan and the Soviet Union). 1965.

Nisso To-O Boeki Kai (ed.). *Nisso boeki yoran nenhan 1959.* (Japan-Soviet trade survey yearbook). 1958.

Norin Keizai Kenkyujo. *Hokuyo gyogyo soran* (A general survey of the Northern Fisheries). 1960.

Oikawa Teisaku. *Nihon shakaito to hoppo ryodo mondai* (The Japanese Socialist Party and the Northern Territorial problem). Mimeographed. 1967.

Petrov Dimitri. *Nisso koryu* (Soviet-Japanese exchanges). 1967.

Oka Yoshitake. *Gendai Nihon no seiji katei* (Political process in modern Japan). 1966.

Okita Saburo. *Nihon keizai no bisshon* (Prospects of the Japanese Economy). 1967.

Sato Tatsuo. *Nihon kenpo seiritsu shi* (History of the formulation of the Japanese Constitution). 2 vols. 1965.

Shinobu Seisaburo. *Sengo Nihon seiji shi* (Political History of Postwar Japan). 4 vols. 1965–68.

Sugimoto Toshio. *Senryo hiroku* (Secret memoirs of the Occupation). 1965.

Watanabe Takeshi. *Senryoka no Nihon zaisei oboekaki* (Japan's financial memoranda during the Occupation period). 1966.

Watanabe Tsuneo. *Habatsu* (Factions). 1960.

Journals and Newspapers:

Akahata.
Asahi.
Asahi Jannaru.
Chuo Koron.
Jiji.
Jiyu.
Kokosaiho gaiko zasshi.
Mainichi.

Nihon Keizai.
Sankei.
Sekai.
Shiso.
Tokyo.
Yumiuri.

WORKS IN ENGLISH

Primary Sources.
a) Government Publications.

Allied Council for Japan. *Corrected Verbatim Record of the Allied Council for Japan.* On microfilm.

Blakeslee, George H. *The Far Eastern Commission: A Study in International Cooperation.* Washington, 1953.

Germany, Foreign Ministry, *Documents on German Foreign Policy 1918–1945.* London, 1949.

International Military Tribunal for the Far East. *Transcript of Proceedings.*

Japan, Economic Planning Agency. *New Long Range Economic Plan of Japan (1961–70): Doubling National Income Plan.* Tokyo, 1961.

Japan, Ministry of Agriculture and Forestry. *SCAP's Memoranda relating to Agricultural Policies of Japan.* Tokyo, 1949.

———. *Collection of SCAP's Memoranda.* Tokyo, 1949.

Japan, Ministry of Foreign Affairs. *Collection of Official Foreign Statements on Japanese Peace Treaty.* 2 vols. Tokyo, 1951.

———. *International Communism and Japan.* Tokyo, 1951.

———. *Documents concerning Allied Occupation and Control of Japan,* vols. 1–5. Tokyo, 1949–1951.

Japan, Ministry of International Trade and Industry. *Foreign Trade White Paper together with a Summary of Economic White Paper, 1958.* Tokyo, 1958.

Japan, Office of Prime Minister, Bureau of Statistics. *Japan Statistical Year Book 1949.*

Pauley, Edwon W. *Report on Japanese Reparations to the President of United States November 1945 to April 1946.* Washington, 1948.

Supreme Commander for Allied Powers. *Political Reorientation of Japan September 1945 to September 1948.* 2 vols. Washington, 1949.

————. *Summation of Non-military Activities in Japan.* (Monthly publication issued from September/October 1945 to September 1948).

United States Congress. *East West Trade Trends: Mutual Defence Assistance Act, 1951, Fourth Report to Congress.* Washington, 1953.

————. *The Strategic Trade Control System 1948–56: Mutual Defence Assistance Control Act, 1951. Ninth Report to Congress.* Washington, 1957.

————. *East West Trade Developments: Tenth Battle Act Report.* Washington, 1958.

United States, Department of Defence. *The Entry of the Soviet Union into the War against Japan, Military Plans, 1941–45.* Washington, 1955.

————. Department of State. *Foreign Relations of the United States, 1931.*

————. *Activities of the Far Eastern Commission: Report by Secretary General February 26, 1946–July 10, 1947.* Washington, 1947.

————. *The Far Eastern Commission: Second Report by the Secretary General July 10, 1947–December 23, 1948.* Washington, 1949.

————. *The Far Eastern Commission: Third Report by the Secretary General December 24, 1948–June 30, 1950.* Washington, 1950.

————. *Occupation of Japan, Policy and Progress.* Washington, 1948.

United States, Department of State, *Conference for the Conclusion and Signature of the Treaty of Peace with Japan, September 4–8, 1951. Record of Proceedings.* Washington, 1951.

————. *United States Relations with Japan, 1945–1952.* (Washington, 1953).

————. *Foreign Relations of the United States: Conferences at Cairo and Tehran.* Washington, 1961.

————. *Foreign Relations of the United States: Conferences at Malta and Yalta.* Washington, 1963.

————. *Conference at Berlin (Potsdam) 1945.* Washington, 1960.

United States, Senate, Foreign Relations Committee. *Hearings 82nd Congress, Second Session, January 21, 22, 23 25, 1952.*

————. *East West Trade: Hearings 88th Congress Second Session, Part I, March-April 1964.*

————. Committee on Banking and Currency. *East West Trade: Parts 1, 2, and 3: Hearings 90th Congress, Second Session, 1968.*

USSR, Ministry of Foreign Affairs. *Correspondence between the Chairman of the Council of Ministers of the USSR and President of the USA and the Prime Minister of Great Britain during the Great Patriotic War of 1941–45.* Moscow, 1957.

b) United Nations Documents

SCOR. Yr. 7, mtgs. 601 and 602; Yr. 10, mtgs. 701–706, 708; Yr. 11, Supplement for October–December 1956.

GAOR. Session 7, plen. mtg. 410; Session 8, plen. mtg. 453; Session 9, plen. mtg. 501; Session 10, plen. mtg. 552; Session 11, supplement no. 17.

General Assembly. A/Conf. 10/5 Rev. 2, A/Conf. 10/6 of June 1955. *Report of the International Technical Conference on the Conservation of Living Resources of the Sea 18 April to 16 May 1955 at Rome.*

c) Other Documents

Columbia University, Russian Institute (ed.). *Anti-Stalin*

Campaign and International Communism—A selection of documents (New York, 1956).

Council of Foreign Relations. *Documents on American Foreign Relations, 1952–*. New York, 1952–.

Ike Nobutaka. *Japan's Decision for War. Record of the 1941 Policy Conferences*. Standford, 1967.

Metzger, Stanley D. *Law of International Trade: Documents and Readings*. Vol. 2 (Washington, 1966).

Royal Institute of International Affairs. *Documents on International Affairs 1936–*. London 1936–.

World Peace Foundation. *Documents on American Foreign Relations, 1936–1951*. Boston 1936–1951.

d) Memoirs and Diaries

Byrnes, J. F. *Speaking Frankly*. London, 1947.
———. *All in One's Lifetime*. New York, 1958.

Churchill, Winston S. *Second World War*. 6 vols. London 1948–1953.

Eden, Anthony. *The Memoirs of Sir Anthony Eden: Full Circle*. London, 1960.

Grew, Joseph C. *Turbulent Era*. 2 vols. London, 1953.

Hull, Cordell. *Memoirs*. 2 vols. New York, 1948.

Kase Toshikazu. *Eclipse of the Rising Sun*. London, 1951.

Leahy, William. *I was there*. London, 1950.

Millis, Walter (ed.). *The Forrestal Diaries*. New York, 1951.

Sherwood, Rober E. (ed.). *The White House Papers of Harry L. Hopkins An Intimate History*. 2 vols. London, 1948.

Shigemitsu Mamoru. *Japan and her Destiny*. London, 1958.

Stimson, Henry L. and McGeorge Bundy. *On Active Service in Peace and War*. New York, 1947.

Togo Shigenori. *The Cause of Japan*. New York, 1956.

Truman, Harry S. *Memoirs*. 2 vols. London, 1955.

Yoshida Shigeru, *The Yoshida Memoirs*. London, 1961.

e) Others

Cole, Allan B. and Nakanishi Naomichi (comp. and ed.).

Japanese Opinion Polls with Socio-Political Significance 1947–1957. Ann Arbor, Michigan, 1959.

Current Digest of the Soviet Press, 1949. New York, 1949–.

Soviet Press Translations, 1946–1949. Washington, 1946–1949.

Secondary Sources
a) Books

Allen, George Cyril. *Japan as a Market and Source of Supply.* Oxford, 1967.

Alperovitz, G. *Atomic Diplomacy: Hiroshima and Potsdam. The Use of Atomic Bomb and the American Confrontation with Soviet Power.* New York, 1965.

Ayusawa, Iwao. *A History of Labour in Modern Japan.* Honolulu, 1966.

Baerwald, Hans. *The Purge of Japanese Leaders under the Occupation.* Berkeley, Los Angeles, 1959.

Ball, W. Macmahon. *Japan—Enemy or Ally.* New York, 1949.

Beasley, W. G. *Select Documents on Japanese Foreign Policy 1853–1868.* London, 1955.

Beloff, Max. *The Foreign Policy of Soviet Russia.* 2 vols., London, 1947–1949.

Bergson, Abram and Simon Kuznets. *Economic Trends in the Soviet Union.* Harvard, 1963.

Borton, Hugh. *American Pre-surrender Planning for Postwar Japan.* New York, 1967.

———. *Japan's Modern Century.* New York, 1955.

Borton et al., *The Far East 1942–46.* London, 1955.

Butow, Robert J. C. *Japan's Decision to Surrender.* Stanford, 1954.

———. *Tojo and the coming of the War.* Princeton, 1961.

Cohen, Bernard C. *The Political Process and Foreign Policy The Making of the Japanese Peace Settlement.* Princeton, 1957.

Dallin, David J. *Soviet Russia and the Far East.* London, 1949.

————. *Soviet Foreign Policy after Stalin.* Philadelphia, 1961.

Deane, John R. *The Strange Alliance.* New York, 1947.

Dennett, Raymond (ed.). *Negotiating with the Russians.* Boston, 1951.

Dunn, F. C. *Peace Making and the Settlement with Japan.* Princeton, 1963.

Fearey, R. A. *Occupation of Japan, Second Phase.* New York, 1950.

Feis, Herbert. *Japan Subdued. The Atomic Bomb and the End of the War in the Pacific.* Princeton, 1961.

————. *Contest over Japan.* New York, 1967.

Fleming, D. F. *The Cold War and Its Origins, 1917–1960.* 2 vols. London, 1961.

Griswold, A. W. *The Far Eastern Policy of the United States.* New York, 1938.

Hellmann, Donald C. *Japanese Foreign Policy and Domestic Politics: the Peace Agreement with the Soviet Union.* Berkeley, 1969.

Hollerman, Leon. *Japan's Dependence on the World Economy; the Approach Toward Economic Liberalisation.* Princeton, 1967.

Huh, Kyung-mo. *Japan's Trade in Asia; Developments Since 1926, Prospects for 1970.* New York, 1966.

Hunsberger, Warren S. *Japan and USA in World Trade.* New York, 1964.

Kajima, Morinosuke. *Modern Japan's Foreign Policy.* Tokyo, 1969.

Kaser, Michael. *COMECON, Integration Problem of the Planned Economies.* London, 1967.

Lensen, George Alexander. *Russia's Japan Expedition of 1852 to 1855.* Gainesville, 1955.

————. *The Russian Push Towards Japan; Russo-Japanese Relations, 1697–1875.* Princeton, 1959.

————. *Japanese Recognition of the USSR; Soviet-Japanese Relations, 1921–1930.* Tokyo, 1970.

————. *The Strange Neutrality: Soviet-Japanese Relations, 1941–1945*. Tallahassee, 1972.

Malozemoff, Andrew. *Russian Far Eastern Policy 1881–1904*. Berkeley, 1958.

Martin, Edwin M. *Aspects of Allied Occupation of Japan*. New York, 1948.

Maxon, Yale Candee. *Control of Japanese Foreign Policy: A Study of Civil Military Rivalry 1930–1945*. Berkeley, 1957.

McNelly, Theodore H. "Domestic and International Influences in Constitutional Revision in Japan," MS, doctoral dissertation. Columbia University, 1952.

Mendel, Douglas H. *The Japanese People and Foreign Policy: A Study of Public Opinion in Post-Treaty Japan*. Berkeley, 1961.

Mikesell, Raymond F. and Jack N. Behrman. *Financing Free World Trade with the Sino-Soviet Bloc*. Princeton, 1958.

Moore, Harriet L. *Soviet Far Eastern Policy 1931–1945*. Princeton, 1945.

Morley, James William. *The Japanese Thrust into Siberia, 1918*. New York, 1957.

————. *Soviet and Communist Chinese Policies towards Japan, 1950–1957. A Comparison*. New York, 1958.

————. *Japan and Korea: America's Allies in the Pacific*. New York, 1965.

Murdoch, James. *A History of Japan*. vol. III. London, 1926.

O'Brien, Frank. *Crisis in World Communism: Marxism in Search of Efficiency*. New York, 1965.

Ogata, Sadako N. *Defiance in Manchuria: The Making of Japanese Foreign Policy*. Berkeley, 1964.

Packard, George R. *Protest in Tokyo: The Security Treaty Crisis of 1960*. Princeton, 1966.

Patterson, Gardner. *Discrimination in International Trade: The Policy Issues 1946–65*. Princeton, 1966.

Presseisen, Ernest L. *Germany and Japan: A Study in Totalitarian Diplomacy*. Hague, 1958.

Rosecrance, R. N. *Australian Diplomacy and Japan 1945–1951*. London, 1962.

Royal Institute of International Affairs. *Survey of International Affairs: Far East 1942–1946*. London, 1955.

Rush, Myron. *Political Succession in USSR*. New York, 1965.

Scalapino, Robert A. *The Japanese Communist Movement 1920–1966*. Berkeley, 1967.

Sebald, William J. *With MacArthur in Japan; A Personal History of the Occupation*. New York, 1965.

Shulman, M. D. *Stalin's Foreign Policy Reappraised*. Harvard, 1964.

Snell, John L. (ed.). *The Meaning of Yalta: Big Three Diplomacy and the New Balance of Power*. Louisiana, 1956.

Stettinus, Edward R., Jr. *Roosevelt and the Russians: The Yalta Conference*. Garden City, 1949.

Stockwin, J. A. A. *The Japanese Socialist Party and Neutralism: A Study of a Political Party and Its Foreign Policy*. Melbourne, 1968.

Swearingen, A. Rodger (ed.).*Soviet and Chinese Communist Power in the World Today*. New York, 1966.

———— and Paul Langer, *Red Flag in Japan*. Stanford, 1952.

Takekoshi, Yosaburo. *The Economic Aspects of the History of the Civilisation of Japan*. vol. 3. London, 1930.

Textor, Robert B. *Failure in Japan*. New York, 1951.

Tucker, Robert C. *The Soviet Political Mind: Studies in Stalinism and Post-Stalin Change*. London, 1963.

United States, Tariff Commission. *Post War Developments in Japan's Foreign Trade*. Washington, 1958.

Whitney, C. *MacArthur: His Rendevous with History*. New York, 1956.

Wildes, Harry Emerson. *Typhoon in Tokyo: The Occupation and Its Aftermath*. New York, 1954.

Yakhontoff, Victor A. *Russia and the Soviet Union in the Far East*. London, 1932.

b) Series

Fuji Bank Bulletin.
The Japan Economic Review. Journal of Social and Political Ideas in Japan.
Royal Institute of International Affairs, London. *Survey of International Affairs.* 1936–.

c) Articles

Borton, Hugh. "Preparation for the Occupation of Japan," *Journal of Asian Studies,* vol. 25, February 1966.

Dore, R. P. "Left and Right in Japan," *International Affairs,* vol. 32, January 1956.

Hitchcock, David I., Jr. "Joint Development of Siberia: Decision-Making in Japanese-Soviet Relations," *Asian Survey,* vol. 10, no. 3 (March 1971).

Ishimoto, Yasuo. "The Northern Territories and a Peace Treaty with the USSR," *Annual Review* (Japan Institute of International Affairs), vol. 4, 1965–68.

Langer, Paul and Rodger Swearingen. "The Japanese Communist Party, the Soviet Union and Korea," *Pacific Affairs,* vol. 23, December 1950.

Lee, Chao-Jin. "The Politics of Sino-Japanese Trade Relations, 1963–1968," *Pacific Affairs,* vol. 42, summer 1968.

May, Ernest R. "The United States, the Soviet Union and the Far Eastern War, 1941–1945," *Pacific Historical Review,* vol. 24, May 1955.

McNelly, Theodore. "The Japanese Constitution, Child of the Cold War," *Political Science Quarterly,* vol. 74, June 1959.

Mieczowski, Z. "The Soviet Far East: Problem Region of the USSR," *Pacific Affairs,* vol. 61, no. 2, 1968.

Morley, James William. "The Soviet-Japanese Peace Declaration," *Political Science Quarterly,* vol. 74, September 1957.

Morley, James William. "Japan's Image of the Soviet Union," *Pacific Affairs,* vol. 37, no. 1 (spring 1962).

Morris, I. I. "Soviet-Japanese Peace Treaty Talks," *The World Today,* vol. 11, August 1955.

————. "Japan and the Moscow Negotiations with the Soviet Union," *The World Today,* vol. 12, November 1956.

————. "Politics in Japan," *The World Today,* vol. 13, March 1957.

Mosley, Philip (ed.). "The Soviet Union Since World War II," *Annals* (American Academy of Political and Social Sciences), vol. 263, May 1949.

Nagano, Shigeo. "Russo-Japanese Trade," *Japan Quarterly,* October-December 1967.

Omori, Shigeo. "Realignment of the JCP," *Japan Quarterly,* October-December 1967.

————. "Japan's Northern Territories," *Japan Quarterly,* January-March 1970.

Shimizu, Minoru. "Japan-Soviet Relations," *Japan Times Weekly.* 15 May 1971.

————. "Soviet Overtures: Efforts to Head Off Rapprochement with Mainland China," *Japan Times Weekly,* 11 September 1971.

Stockwin, J. A. A. "The Communist Party of Japan," *Problems of Communism,* vol. 16, January-February 1967.

Stockwin, J. A. A. "Is Japan a Post-Marxist Society?" *Pacific Affairs,* vol. 41, Summer 1968.

————. "Foreign Policy Perspectives of the Japanese Left: Confrontation or Consensus," *Pacific Affairs,* vol. 42, Winter 1969–70.

Vinacke, Harold M. "The Growth of an Independent Foreign Policy in Japan," *Pacific Affairs,* vol. 38, Spring 1965.

Ward, Robert E. "The Origins of the Present Japanese Constitution," *The American Political Science Review,* vol. 50, December 1956.

Index

189

THE DIPLOMATIC PRESS, INC.

1102 BETTON ROAD, TALLAHASSEE, FLORIDA 32303, U.S.A.

Satow, Sir Ernest. *Korea and Manchuria between Russia and Japan 1895–1904. The Observations of Sir Ernest Satow, British Minister and Plenipotentiary to Japan and China.* Selected and edited with a historical introduction by George Alexander Lensen. First published 1966; second printing 1968. 300 pp., collotype frontispiece, cloth. ISBN 0–910512–01–9. $12.50.
". . . a welcome addition to primary source material for the study of Far Eastern diplomatic history."—*The Journal of Asian Studies*
". . . full of interesting and illuminating views from a diplomat of experience and wisdom. . ."—*The American Historical Review*

D'Anethan, Baron Albert. *The D'Anethan Dispatches from Japan 1894–1910. The Observations of Baron Albert D'Anethan, Belgian Minister Plenipotentiary and Dean of the Diplomatic Corps.* Translated and edited with a historical introduction by George Alexander Lensen. 1967. 272 pp., collotype frontispiece, cloth. ISBN 0–910512–02–7 $15.00.
"A companion volume to . . . Sir Ernest Satow . . . Masterfully selected excerpts of heretofore unpublished official dispatches . . ."—*Historische Zeitschrift*
"Valuable to students in East Asian international relations."—*Choice*

Lensen, George Alexander. *The Russo-Chinese War.* 1967. 315 pp., collotype frontispiece, maps, extensive bibliography, cloth. ISBN 0–910512–03–05. $15.00. "The first full-length treatment of Sino-Russian hostilities in Manchuria during the Boxer Rebellion of 1900 . . . Lensen writes clearly, vividly, and with full mastery of his subject."—*Choice*

Will, John Baxter. *Trading Under Sail off Japan 1860–1899. The Recollections of Captain John Baxter Will, Sailing-Master and Pilot.* Edited with a historical introduction by George Alexander Lensen. 1968. 190 pp., lavishly printed and illustrated, cloth. ISBN 0–910512–04–3 $12.50.
". . . this extremely interesting story . . . ranks with the few which, while not perhaps of the type to keep young children from play, should keep most men 'in the chimney corner.'"—*The Japan Times*

Lensen, George Alexander (comp.). *Japanese Diplomatic and Consular Officials in Russia. A Handbook of Japanese Representatives in Russia from 1874 to 1968.* 230 pp., hardcover. ISBN 0–910512–05–1. $15.00.
"A useful handbook for every serious student of the relations between Japan and the U.S.S.R." *Narody Azii i Afriki*

Lensen, George Alexander (comp.). *Russian Diplomatic and Consular Officials in East Asia. A Handbook of the Representatives of Tsarist Russia and the Provisional Government in China, Japan and Korea from 1858 to 1924 and of Soviet Representatives in Japan from 1925 to 1968.* 1968. 294 pp., hard-cover. ISBN 0–910512–06–X $15.00.
"The two handbooks are essential reference works for every library of East Asian or Russian history; for specialists in the field of Russian-East Asian relations where the author is known as a distinguished

pioneering scholar, they will be indispensable companions."—*Pacific Affairs*

Westwood, J.N. *Witnesses of Tsushima* 1970. xiv, 321 pp. plus 38 illustrations, cloth, ISBN 0–910512–08–06 $15.00.
"Dr. Westwood, by interweaving his own narrative with eyewiness accounts and the official reports both Russian and Japanese gives us a far more accurate version of the famous Russian voyage out of Kronstadt to the Straits of Tsushima and the subsequent battle than has been available heretofore."—*Journal of Asian Studies*

Lensen, George Alexander. *Japanese Recognition of the U.S.S.R.; Soviet-Japanese Relations 1921–1930.* 425 pp. illustrated, cloth. ISBN 0–910512–09–4. $15.00.
"The book is a careful detailed treatment of an important period in Russo-Japanese relations. It will be of special interest to diplomatic and economic historians and of more general interest to those concerned with Japan's position in East Asia or the Soviet Union's relations there."—*Choice*

McNally, Raymond T. *Chaadayev and his Friends. An Intellectual History of Peter Chaadayev and his Russian Contemporaries.* 1971, about 285 pp., frontispiece, imitation leather. ISBN 0–910512–11–6. $15.00.
A new and highly readable interpretation of the place of Peter Chaadayev (1794-1856), the first Russian Westernizer and a unique thinker, in intellectual history, based on research in Soviet archives.

Poutiatine, Countess Olga. *War and Revolution. Excerpts from the Letters and Diaries of the Countess Olga Poutiatine.* Translated and edited by George Alexander Lensen. 1971, about 150 pp., illustrated, cloth. ISBN 0–910512–12–4. $12.50.
A moving eyewitness account of the Russian Revolution and of conditions in Russian and Anglo-Russian military hospitals during the First World War by the granddaughter of the Russian admiral who competed with Commodore Perry in the opening of Japan.

Sansom, Lady Katharine. *Sir George Sansom and Japan.* A memoir of Sir George Sansom, G. B. E., K. C. M. G., Diplomat Historian, by his wife. Late 1971 or early 1972, about 150 pp., illustrated, cloth. ISBN 0–910512–13–2. $15.00.
The diplomatic and scholarly life of Sir George Sansom, the foremost Western authority on Japan, mirrored in the letters and diary entries of his wife and himself, with unforgettable thumbnail sketches of leading diplomatic, political, military and literary figures in Japan from 1928–1950.

Kutakov, Leonid N. *Japanese Foreign Policy on the Eve of the Pacific War. A Soviet View.* 1972. 256 pp., frontispiece, cloth. ISBN 910512–15–0. $15.00.
". . . a tightly knit interpretation of an epochal aspect of modern history (particularly the long essay on Japanese-Russian relations) which will intrigue students of the background of World War II."—*Library Journal.*

Lensen, George Alexander. *The Strange Neutrality: Soviet-Japanese Relations During the Second World War, 1941–1945.* 1972. 335 pp., illustrated, cloth. ISBN 910512–14–0. $15.00.

Vishwanathan, Savitri. *Normalization of Japanese-Soviet Relations 1945–1970*. About 200 pp. illustrated, cloth. ISBN 910512–14–0. $15.00.
A study by an Indian scholar, based primarily on Japanese sources.

Lensen, George Alexander. *The Damned Inheritance: The Soviet Union and the Manchurian Crises, 1924–1935*. About 500 pp., illustrated, cloth. ISBN 910512–17–5. $19.80.
An account of the triangular Russo-Chinese-Japanese struggle over Manchuria and the Chinese Eastern Railway and of American and British reaction thereto.

*   *   *

Lensen, George Alexander. *Faces of Japan: A Photographic Study*. 154 large collotype reproductions, beautifully printed in a limited edition. 1968. 312 pp., cloth. ISBN 0–910512–07–8. $30.00.
Candid portraits of Japanese of all walks of life at work and at play.

Lensen, George Alexander. *April in Russia: A Photographic Study*. 100 large collotype reproductions, beautifully printed in a limited edition. 1970. 208 pp., cloth. ISBN 0–910512–10–8. $35.00 (originally $40.00).